An American Journey

Life Lessons for Parents on Immigrant Children

Bhagwan Satiani

HAMl

A 1

The Rowman & Litt

Lanham • Boulder • New   *...ymouth, UK*

This book is dedicated to my wife and best friend Mira, children Anmol and Anand, daughter-in-law Nidhi, grandson Roshan, my parents Sobhraj and Lachmi Satiani and my mother-in-law Ganga Parwani.

A special dedication to the land of the free and the home of the brave.

Contents

Illustrations

FIGURES

TABLES

Preface

How does a person get to be this lucky or blessed? I have asked myself that question many times.

I do not know the answer.

I have been blessed with a wonderful family and the best children a father could possibly ask for. I looked around at my children's friends when they were growing up and became acutely aware of how special our children were. This included their South Asian friends (who were few) and non-Asians as well. I often thought to myself: What did we do right and what did we do wrong? What lessons have I learned that I might pass on to other immigrants? Good fortune and a blessed life cannot be passed on, but experiences can. I started to look for similar books, but the few books written have been more about explaining U.S. customs and laws to immigrants rather than offering advice on rearing children. So that was the motivation behind this book.

My specific experiences related to my South Asian background may be somewhat unique to that specific culture. However, I would venture to say that the lessons in this book apply to most, if not all, immigrants to the U.S. or other Western countries from various parts of the world. This is because a thread of insecurity—concern with losing touch with our own culture and anxiety about our children failing in a foreign land—runs through the thoughts of all immigrants. The challenges in raising children are also common to most immigrant groups. How do we balance educating children about our own culture with encouraging them to fit in with local customs? How do we allow them to enjoy the numerous freedoms here and yet instill respect for our traditions at home? These concerns are common to most immigrant families.

The first chapter lays out the enormous change in the population mix that will occur in the U.S. over the next few decades. Chapter 2 deals with common issues arising at home, including raising children, assimilation problems, language barriers, privacy conflicts, and disagreements between parents and children. Chapter 3 on values considers how to address racist behavior that may be aimed toward your children. We will also discuss the importance of keeping money in proper perspective, teaching empathy and pride in a child's own ethnicity and instructing children about frugality and individual responsibility. Chapter 4 on education emphasizes the importance of education in immigrant families and how education can become a source of conflict because of the high standards set by parents. There is discussion of grading systems, college savings plans, career choices, and risk avoidance common in immigrant parents.

The role of the strongest allies of most immigrant parents other family members and friends, is highlighted in Chapter 5. Choosing a life partner, dating, questions about sex, divorce, and living together are looked at in Chapter 6. We will face the biggest source of serious conflict within immigrant families, children marrying outside their ethnic/racial/religious group. Another source of friction between parent's and children is when the children are either ambivalent or not in tune with their parents' faith. Faith and religion are dealt with in Chapter 7. Finally, the epilogue gives the reader my sense of how I view the changes in the U.S. over the last forty years and why I truly believe in my adopted land.

Millions of teenagers will arrive in North America or born of new immigrants here over the next few decades. A recent U.S. Census report indicates that babies born to minorities now outnumber those born to whites. A lot of these minority parents are immigrants. Parents of these young children born in the U.S. or arriving here need some guidance on how to prepare to deal with conflicts that will surely arise in the family. I am hopeful that this book will provide some assistance to parents and their children alike. The parents may learn to anticipate issues that my family has experienced and their children may begin to comprehend the basis of their parents' concerns.

I have no special talent for writing a non-scientific book. All the mistakes in the book are mine. When illustrating points with anecdotes, names and facts have been changed so that I would not violate confidentiality, but if I have at some point, I ask your forgiveness.

I have borrowed real events in the families of my siblings, other family members and friends, particularly our cluster of close friends of over thirty years. I am grateful to my brothers Suresh and Haresh and my sister Neelam and their children for their regard and respect that I may or may not have deserved. Finally, my sincere thanks to Paul Ingram for assistance with editing the manuscript.

I wish you the reader the best and hope you will have the same good fortune my wife and I have had.

God Bless you and God Bless the United States of America.

Chapter One

The Scope of Immigration in the United States

Although its precise origin is disputed, the name *America* was apparently bestowed by German map maker Martin Waldseemüller as a mark of respect for Amerigo Vespucci, an Italian explorer.[1] It is also speculated that three ships, with an Italian captain in charge, discovered America while sailing under a Spanish flag.

The name *United States of America* was fashioned after "The United States of the Netherlands." Dutch immigrants also brought with them such every day items as waffles, cookies, doughnuts, as well as sports like boating, golfing, bowling, and ice-skating.[2]

Immigration from various countries to the U.S. has varied considerably depending on the time in history, the political forces prevailing at the time, the need for skilled workers and U.S. involvement in foreign wars (Table 1). There are many reasons why the U.S. has had a variable policy on immigration. Most of the reasons are political, having to do with the phase of history, the general economic state, or a recent war. In peace time, the long-term view generally prevails. This view is based upon how many new immigrant workers the country needs to satisfy the needs of the U.S.

Table 1. Landmarks in U.S. Immigration

Year	Event
1607	English colonists found Virginia.
1619	First Negro slaves arrive.
1620	The Mayflower ship arrives with pilgrims.
1630	Puritans migrate to New England area.
1654	Jewish settlers arrive from Brazil to escape Portuguese persecution.
1681	Quakers find and settle in Pennsylvania.

(continued)

Table 1. *(continued)*

Year	Event
1683	German settlers arrive in Pennsylvania.
1707	Scottish immigrants arrive.
1718	Large number of Scottish and Irish immigrants.
1740	Naturalization Act passed, conferring British citizenship on alien immigrants.
1825	First Norwegian immigrants arrive.
1830	Polish immigrants arrive as a result of Polish Revolution, allotted land in Illinois. German, Italian, and Swedish migration starts.
1846	Large Irish immigration as a result of potato famine. The Irish constitute 44% of foreign-born population by 1850.
1882	Federal immigration law bans entry of mentally challenged ("idiots, lunatics").
	Chinese Exclusion Act also bans Chinese laborers from entering.
1886	Statue of Liberty dedicated.
1892	Ellis Island becomes a reception point for immigrants.
1921	New law establishes quotas favoring Northern and Western Europeans, based on a 1920 census and fixing new immigrant numbers based on existing national origin (the National Origins System).
1924	National Origins Act fixes number of immigrants allowed with quotas.
1940	Under Alien Registration Act, all aliens (non-U.S. citizens) within the United States must register with the government and receive an Alien Registration Receipt Card (later called the "Green Card").
1929	Quota system allows unlimited immigration from Western Hemisphere.
1945	Puerto Ricans immigrate in large numbers.
1948	Displaced Person Act (amended in 1950) allows 400,000 refugees to enter over four years.
1952	Immigration and Naturalization Act (McCarran-Walter Act) upholds the national origins quota system established by the 1924 Act, allowing the national origins formula. Although it ends exclusion of Asians from immigrating, severe quotas are put into place for those from the Asian-Pacific triangle.
1953-56	Large immigration from Hungary and ""Iron Curtain" countries.
1960	Large influx of refugees from Cuba.
1965	Hart-Celler Act in 1965 replaces the quota system with preference categories based more on family relationships and job skills, giving preference to potential immigrants with relatives in the United States and to those with occupations deemed critical by the U.S. Department of Labor.
1968	Immigration discrimination based on race, place of birth, sex and residence eliminated. Restrictions on Oriental US immigration abolished.
1976	Preferential treatment for residents of the Western Hemisphere eliminated.
1986	Immigration Act legalizes thousands of illegal immigrants, introducing sanctions on employers for hiring illegal workers and including tough laws to prevent fraudulent marriages.
2003	The Immigration and Naturalization Service (INS) becomes part of the U.S. Department of Homeland Security.

The world's developed and under developed countries are all going through a transition influenced by variations in mortality and birth rates.[3]

The Pareto Principle or "80:20 rule" applies here also. This rule of thumb, named after an Italian economist, states that 80 percent of results are based on 20 percent of causes. In this case, developing countries are 80 percent of the population and produce about 20 percent of the gross output of the world and vice versa for the developed countries. The U.S. has a higher birth rate in comparison with other developed countries partly because it allows more immigrants, who tend to have more children than natives. Population estimates indicate that the U.S. population will climb from 296 million in 2005 to 438 million in 2050, and 82 percent of the increase will be due to immigrants and their descendants.[4]

Overall, the most immigrants have come from European countries, with a large peak occurring in the 1990-1999 time period (Figure 1).[5] However, since 1960, immigrants from Mexico have been by far the largest group to have come to the U.S. According to 2000 U.S. census figures, foreign born residents (those who were born outside the U.S., regardless of their citizenship status) numbered 31,107,890. Of that total, 12,542,625 were U.S. citizens and 18,565,265 were non-citizens. Over half (51 percent) came from Latin America (Mexico, Central and South America, and the Caribbean), 26 percent came from Asia, 16 percent came from European countries and the rest came from other countries (for example, Canada, Africa, and Oceania). In terms of countries of origin, the top ten countries were, in descending order: Mexico, China, Philippines, India, Vietnam, Cuba, Korea, Canada, El Salvador, and Germany.[6]

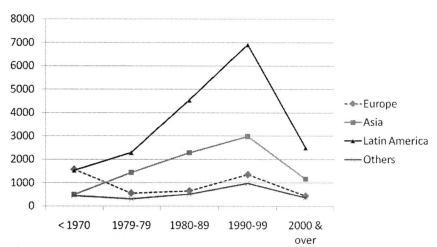

Figure 1. Foreign-born population by origin and arrival (in thousands, 2003 data). From "A Description of the Immigrant Population," Congressional Budget Office, November 2004. Data from Department of Commerce, Census Bureau, Current Population Survey: Annual Social and Economic Supplement, 2003.http://cbo.gov/ftpdocs/60xx/doc6019/11-23-Immigrant.pdf.

The foreign born population tends to be older (38.4 versus 35.1 years) than the native population. However, this is distorted by the fact that there are three times fewer people under eighteen in the foreign born group. Japanese had the highest median age (44.1 years) and Asian Indians had the lowest (31.7 years).[7]

The Asian population in the U.S. will grow from 14 million people in 2005 to 41 million in 2050. As a percentage of the total population, Asians have grown from a mere 0.6 percent of the population in 1960 to 5 percent in 2005. It is estimated that they will comprise 9 percent by 2050. In 2005, 58 percent of Asians in the U.S. were foreign born but by 2050 less than half (47 percent) will be foreign born.[8]

The Chinese make up the largest component of the Asian population in the United States today. About one-third of foreign born Asians entered the U.S. during the 1990s and about 17 percent arrived in 2000 or later. A total of 50 percent arrived in the U.S. after 1990.[9]

The racial composition of immigrants, according to the 2000 census, consists of: 43 percent white, 22.5 percent Asian, 6.8 percent black or African American, and the rest were of more than one race or other races. Eighty-three percent spoke a language other than English at home, with 43.4 percent speaking Spanish and 18 percent Asian languages.

IMMIGRATION TRENDS

Immigration to the U.S. picked up in the early 1900s and then slowed considerably between World War I and II . Following World War II, immigration picked up again and, except for small variations, has remained steady. The migration rate into the U.S. has varied from 0.3 to 16.5 (average 4.4) per 1000 U.S. residents, depending on the time period. At this writing, the recent migration rate has hovered around 4.8 per 1000 U.S. residents.

The Congressional Budget Office reported that the 33 million foreign born persons living in the U.S. in 2003 represented 12 percent of the U.S. population. (Figure 2) That is the highest share since 1930.[10] Two-thirds of immigrants have been residents of the U.S. for over ten years and one-third for over twenty years (Figure 3).[11] Furthermore, half of the foreign born persons have arrived since 1990 and over 1 million new immigrants enter the U.S. each year, accounting for over one-third of the population growth between 1990 and 2000.[12] More than two-thirds of new immigrants are sponsored by family members and granted entry because they are spouses, children, or parents of U.S. citizens.[13]

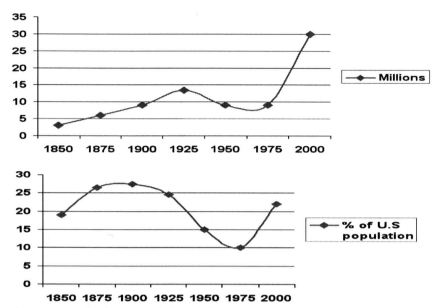

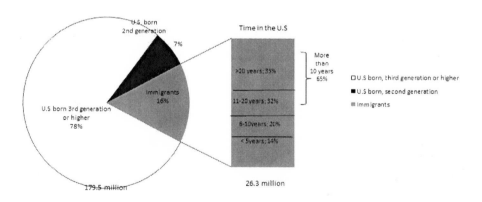

Figure 2. Foreign-born population of the U.S., 1850-2000. Adapted from Congressional Budget Office.

Figure 3. Immigrants as a share of the non-elderly adult population and by length of time in the U.S., 2007. From Peter Cunningham and Samantha Artiga, "How Does Health Coverage and Access to Care for Immigrants Vary by Length of Time in the U.S.? Executive Summary," Kaiser Commission on Medicaid and the Uninsured, The Henry J. Kaiser Family Foundation, June 2009. Available at www.kff.org/uninsured/upload/7916_ES.pdf. This information was reprinted with permission from the Henry J. Kaiser Family Foundation. The Kaiser Family Foundation is a non-profit private operating foundation, based in Menlo Park, California, dedicated to producing and communicating the best possible analysis and information on health issues.

SPECIFIC IMMIGRANT GROUPS

Asian immigrants are far from homogenous and have origins that spread across the Far East, Southeast Asia, and the Indian sub-continent. This large group includes different cultures and many languages and dialects (Table 2).

The Chinese were the first Asians to arrive in the U.S. in large numbers. In the 1830s, Chinese were working in the Hawaiian sugarcane fields and selling their goods in New York City. Later in the mid 1800s the discovery of gold brought many Chinese to California. The Chinese worked in farming, built levees, gardened, cooked, and managed orchards.[14]

However, the Immigration Act of 1917 stopped legal Chinese immigration almost entirely due to local prejudice. Specifically, the Chinese Exclusion Act resulted in thousands of immigrants returning to China. The Chinese population in the U.S. fell to a lowly 62,000 people in 1920.[15]

Other Asian groups also immigrated in the early 1900s. Most minorities, because of their great success and hard work, faced discrimination by legislation that barred non-citizens from owning or leasing land.[16] In 1946, however, passage of the Luce-Celler Bill allowed immigrants to become citizens through naturalization.[17] A second wave started after passage of the Immigration and Naturalization Act, which made it easier for skilled Asians to enter in the mid-1960s.

Table 2. Asian Household Population by Detailed Group: 2004

Detailed group	Population	% of Asian alone population
Asian alone	12,097,281	100%
Asian Indian	2,245,239	18.6%
Bangladeshi	50,473	0.4%
Cambodian	195,208	1.6%
Chinese, except Taiwanese	2,829,627	23.4%
Filipino	2,148,227	17.8%
Hmong	163,733	1.4%
Indonesian	52,267	0.4%
Japanese	832,039	6.9%
Korean	1,251,092	10.3%
Laotian	226,661	1.9%
Malaysian	11,458	0.1%
Pakistani	208,852	1.7%
Sri Lankan	22,339	0.2%
Taiwanese	70,771	0.6%
Thai	130,548	1.1%
Vietnamese	1,267,510	10.5%
Other Asian	250,666	2.1%

From U.S Census Bureau, 2004 American Community Survey, Selected population Profiles.

Immigrants from the Philippines are the third largest immigrant group in the U.S., with over 1.4 million people. Half of all immigrants from the Philippines live in California, mostly in Southern California. Almost one quarter of all foreign born soldiers serving in the armed forces are from the Philippines.[18] Over 90 percent are Christian Malays, with the rest belonging to various other faiths.[19] Large segments of the Philippine population migrated as farm workers in the early 1900s.

The early immigrants (85 percent Sikhs and 10-12 percent Muslims) from South Asia were farmers and agriculturists from the province of Punjab in India, who settled in California in the mid-nineteenth century.[20] The Immigration Act of 1917 stopped new immigrants for many years, and due to a dearth of South Asian women, Punjabi men often married their laborer women of Mexican ancestry. The largest wave of South Asian immigration occurred after the passage of the Immigration and Naturalization Act in 1965. Under this legislation, visas were issued on the basis of quotas for each country (approximately 20,000), taking into consideration preferred skills and efforts to promote re-unification of families. As a result, the initial group was from the professional and educated class, followed by relatives of migrants. This group of immigrants was more diverse and included people from Pakistan, Nepal, Bangla Desh, Sri Lanka, and Afghanistan. These immigrants tended to settle in large metropolitan areas, and 70 percent are settled in New York, California, New Jersey, Texas, Pennsylvania, Michigan, Illinois, and Ohio.[21]

Japanese immigrants came to Hawaii (before it became a state of the U.S.) in the late 1800s as contract laborers but progressed to become tenants in land cultivation. They then gravitated to the West Coast as laborers in farms, mines, and the railroads until the Immigration Act of 1924 stopped almost all immigration. After this period, almost all second-generation Japanese (or "Nisie" as they were called) became totally "Americanized' and fully integrated.[22] However, this commitment to their new land was to be tested after Pearl Harbor and World War II in February of 1942, when President Roosevelt issued Executive Order 9066, condemning almost 125,000 Japanese Americans to interment in "concentration" camps. A 100 years or so later, the over 1 million Japanese Americans are a vital part of the U.S.

The 120 Korean immigrants on the *S.S. Gaelic* arriving into Honolulu Harbor in 1903 were the first wave of Korean immigration.[23] The next wave came as a result of the War Brides Act of 1946, so that when the Korean War came, Korean women married to American servicemen were allowed to come to the U.S. The final wave came as a result of the Immigration Act of 1965, which opened the door for Asian immigrants.

Occupational and Economic Status

Education is probably the single most important determining factor in the degree of success achieved by immigrants. Approximately, 29 percent of immigrants have less than a high school education. Management, professional or other related occupations were listed by 28.4 percent of immigrants, service occupations by 20 percent, and sales and office occupations by another 20 percent. Remaining immigrants listed a variety of other occupations and skills. About 46 percent of civilian Asians over the age of sixteen worked in management, professional, and related occupations, compared to 38 percent of non-Hispanic whites.[24] Asian Indian immigrants are more likely to be in these occupations (61 percent) compared to Chinese (52 percent) and Japanese (48 percent).

In terms of distribution, immigrants are weighted towards both sides of the spectrum. A much larger share than the native population is at either of two extremes. They tend to possess either an advanced degree, or they lack a high school diploma.[25] Latin American immigrants tend to have much less education compared to Asians. About 85 percent of Asian immigrants are high school graduates. Half the Asian population has a college degree and 19 percent an advanced degree. Only 12 percent of the Latino group has an advanced degree.[26] Two thirds of Asian Indians have a bachelor's degree or more education. This explains the lower than average earnings in the immigrant population compared to natives, although this changes over time. The median income of families with a foreign-born head was about $43,000, which is about 79 percent of the median income of a native headed family. There are significant differences in socio-economic status and employment status depending on the length of time immigrants have resided in the U.S. (Figure 4). A current study of immigrants has put the family income of more recent immigrants at 57 percent of average ($37,000) compared to 95 percent of the U.S. average ($64,000) for immigrants who have been in the U.S. for over twenty years.[27]

As mentioned, the Asian immigrants bring a higher level of education, and their median income is higher than that of native citizens. Asian Indians and Filipinos have the highest median family income, which is on average $10,000 higher than other Asian households. The median value of Asian owner occupied homes is $306,000, twice the value ($154,000) of homes owned by non-Hispanic whites.

In general, immigrant households' use of the welfare system is higher for most programs compared to native Americans. However, most immigrant households do not use the welfare system. In the American Community Survey in 2004, 12 percent of Asians were living below the poverty level, compared to 9 percent of non-Hispanic whites.[28] The poverty rate was highest among Koreans, Vietnamese, and Chinese.[29] In 2002, more foreign born

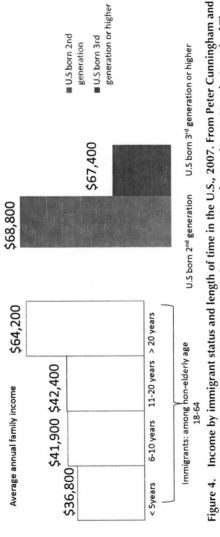

Average annual family income

$36,800 $41,900 $42,400 $64,200

< 5years   6-10 years   11-20 years   > 20 years

Immigrants: among non-elderly age 18-64

$68,800

$67,400

U.S born 2nd generation   U.S born 3rd generation or higher

■ U.S born 2nd generation
■ U.S born 3rd generation or higher

Figure 4.   Income by immigrant status and length of time in the U.S., 2007. From Peter Cunningham and Samantha Artiga, "How Does Health Coverage and Access to Care for Immigrants Vary by Length of Time in the U.S.? Executive Summary," Kaiser Commission on Medicaid and the Uninsured, The Henry J. Kaiser Family Foundation, June 2009. Available at www.kff.org/uninsured/upload/7916_ES.pdf. This information was reprinted with permission from the Henry J. Kaiser Family Foundation. The Kaiser Family Foundation is a non-profit private operating foundation, based in Menlo Park, California, dedicated to producing and communicating the best possible analysis and information on health issues.

residents were living below the poverty level (16.6 percent versus 11.5 percent) or unemployed (7.5 percent versus 6.2 percent) compared to the native population.[30]

The earlier second generation immigrants (late 1990s) following the Immigration and Naturalization Act in 1965, started to show evidence of lower socio-economic status. In 1995, a study showed that California had one of the highest percentages of Asian Indian American children deemed to be living in poverty.[31]

The heaviest concentration of immigrants is in six states (California, Texas, New York, Florida, Illinois, and New Jersey). Forty percent of immigrants live in metropolitan areas in contrast to only 27 percent of the native population.[32] Almost two out of three Asians are married, compared to 57 percent of non-Hispanic whites.[33]

CITIZENSHIP STATUS

The 2008 American Community Survey, conducted by the U.S. Census Bureau, indicated that, of the 38 million foreign born living in the U.S. (12.5 percent of the population in 2008), 43 percent or 16 million were naturalized citizens (Table 3). Citizenship status varies according to the length of time the immigrants have resided in the U.S. About 48 percent and 65 percent of those in the U.S. for more than ten and twenty years, respectively, are U.S. citizens.[34] The younger immigrants tend not to be citizens.

Table 3.   Foreign-born Naturalized Residents of the U.S.

	United States	
	Estimate	%
Total:	37,960,935	
Not a U.S. citizen	21,631,026	57%
Naturalized citizens:	16,329,909	43%
Naturalized 2006 or later	2,272,348	
Naturalized 2001 to 2005	3,098,150	
Naturalized 1996 to 2000	3,411,696	
Naturalized 1991 to 1995	1,844,192	
Naturalized 1986 to 1990	1,518,796	
Naturalized 1981 to 1985	1,084,481	
Naturalized before 1981	3,100,246	

From U.S. Census Bureau, 2008 American Community Survey.

In 2004, the U.S. Census Bureau reported that about half of all Asians lived in three states, California, New York, and Texas.[35]

One of the most fascinating discourses on Americans to date is the observations by Alexis de Tocqueville, a French aristocrat and political scientist who, along with a friend, came to America in 1831 to learn about American life. His book *Democracy in America* (Vol. 1, 1835; Vol. 2, 1840) is a classic in terms of his brilliant observations about U.S. and world culture and politics.[36] One passage stands out in explaining the core foundational reason why immigrants are attracted to the U.S. "In America, where the privileges of birth never existed, and where riches confer no peculiar rights on their possessors, men unacquainted with each other are very ready to frequent the same places, and find neither peril nor advantage in the free interchange of their thoughts."[37] Immigrants have formed the backbone of this nation, following the extraordinary effort by the English Pilgrims in the early seventeenth century. They will continue to come to "the land of the free and the home of the brave" as long as this country stands for the principles on which it was founded.

OUT MIGRATION

Out migration is the return of immigrants to their home countries. It is estimated that about 280,000 immigrants return to their country of origin each year.[38] Although, the impression is that the recent economic downturn or 9/11 has led to more out migration, the numbers seem to have remained fairly steady.

NOTES

1. John R. Hébert, "The Map that Named America," Library of Congress (Sept., 2003), http://www.loc.gov/loc/lcib/0309/maps.html.

2. J. F. Kennedy, *A Nation of Immigrants* (New York: Harper & Row, 1986).

3. Congressional Budget Office, "Global Population Aging in the 21st Century and Its Economic Implications" (December 2005), http://www.cbo.gov/ftpdocs/69xx/doc6952/12-12-Global.pdf.

4. Jeffrey Passel and D'Vera Cohn, "Immigration to Play Lead Role in Future U.S. Growth," Pew Research Center (Feb. 11, 2008), http://www.pewresearch.org/pubs/729/united-states-population-projections.

5. "A Description of the Immigrant Population," Congressional Budget Office (November 2004), http://www.cbo.gov/ftpdocs/60xx/doc6019/11-23-Immigrant.pdf.

6. N. Malone, "The Foreign Born Population: 2000," Census 2000 brief, U.S. Census Bureau (December 2003).

7. "The American Community—Asians: 2004," American Community Survey Reports, U.S. Census Bureau (Feb., 2007), http://www.census.gov/prod/2007pubs/acs-05.pdf.

8. "Foreign-Born Profiles," U.S. Census Bureau, http://www.census.gov/population/www/socdemo/foreign/STP-159-2000tl.html.

9. "The American Community—Asians: 2004."

10. "Description of the Immigrant Population."

11. Peter Cunningham, and Samantha Artiga, "How Does Health Coverage and Access to Care for Immigrants Vary by Length of Time in the U.S.?" Kaiser Commission on Medicaid and the Uninsured, http//www.kff.org/uninsured/upload/7916_ES.pdf.

12. Description of the Immigrant Population.

13. Ibid.

14. K. I. Leonard, *The South Asian American* (Westport, CT: Greenwood, 1997), 40.

15. "Immigration, the Journey to America, the Chinese," Oracle Education Foundation, http://library.thinkquest.org/20619/Chinese.html.

16. Leonard, *South Asian American*, 41.

17. Ibid., 47.

18. Elizabeth Grieco, "The Foreign Born from the Philippines in the United States," Migration Information Source (Nov. 2003), http://www.migrationinformation.org/Feature/display.cfm?ID=179#1.

19. Republic of the Philippines Web site, "General Information," http://www.gov.ph/index.php?option=com_content&task=view&id=200020&Itemid=26.

20. Leonard, *South Asian American*, 43.

21. Ibid., 68.

22. "Immigration . . . Japanese," Library of Congress, http://memory.loc.gov/learn//features/immig/japanese3.html.

23. "Korean American History," http://apa.si.edu/Curriculum%20Guide-Final/unit1.htm.

24. U.S. Department of Homeland Security, Office of Immigration Statistics, www.census.gov/compendia/statab/2010/tables/10s0049.xls.

25. "Description of the Immigrant Population."

26. U.S. Department of Homeland Security, Office of Immigration Statistics, www.census.gov/compendia/statab/2010/tables/10s0049.xls.

27. Steven A. Camarota, "Immigrants at Mid-Decade: A Snapshot of America's Foreign-Born Population in 2005," Center for Immigration Studies (Dec., 2005), http://www.cis.org/articles/2005/back1405.html.

28. "Asian/Pacific American Heritage Month: May 2006," U.S. Census Bureau News (March 27, 2006), http://www.census.gov/newsroom/releases/pdf/cb06-ff06.pdf.

29. "The American Community—Asians: 2004."

30. B. D. Proctor and J. Dalaker, "Poverty in the United States 2002," in *Current Population Reports*, U.S. Census Bureau, 60-222.

31. Leonard, *South Asian American*, 82. India West, August 18, 1995: C1, C 15, C 18; December 15, 1995: A1, A31-32.

32. "The American Community—Asians: 2004."

33. Ibid.

34. Cunningham and Artiga, "How Does Health Coverage and Access to Care for Immigrants Vary by Length of Time in the U.S.?"

35. "The American Community—Asians: 2004."

36. R. D. Heffner, *Democracy in America. Alexis De Tocqueville,* Signet Classic, New American Library (New York: Penguin, 2001).

37. Ibid., 122.

38. Steven A. Camarota, "Immigrants in the United States, 2007, A Profile of America's Foreign-Born Population," Center for Immigration Studies (Nov. 2007), http://www.cis.org/immigrants_profile_2007.

Chapter Two

The Home

Immigrants often arrive in the U.S. with cultural baggage that is packed full of beliefs. These include well-defined gender roles, paternalistic behavior, and conservative social norms.

My family is no exception. The saving grace is that both my wife and I are highly educated and somewhat "westernized" by exposure to books, music, and movies. Nonetheless, it has been difficult to settle in with our baggage filled with a potpourri of social norms. Which part do we lose and which part do we claim as our own? How do we keep the best of both cultures? What follows is some advice on what we kept and what we abandoned.

HOW MUCH ASSIMILATION (OR ACCULTURATION)?

By *assimilation* I mean adaptation, integration, and adjustment to the American culture. All immigrants, even people such as I, who think they are familiar with common customs through the media, are in for some culture shock. But after that initial reaction, the question is not whether we as immigrants can assimilate, but how much should we assimilate? Some immigrants fear that they will lose their own culture so they stay close to like-minded fellow immigrants and try to deal with native citizens only when they have no other choice. Most of us try to teach our children our own customs while encouraging them to mix and learn new customs so as not to be left out. If the children grow up here, they are American. We can hyphenate our origin in whatever fashion we want, calling ourselves "Asian-American" or "Arab-American," but we are American.

There is no question that children undergo significant acculturation stress while growing up in households of first generation immigrants. The Asian

Indian family, for example, considers itself a single unit, not a collection of separate, independent entities. It is considered normal for a grown up adult to remain "dependent" on his or her parents. The identification of an adult based upon complete independence, responsibility, and freedom in Western culture is foreign to the Asian Indian environment.[1]

In the Asian Indian family unit, as well as among other immigrant families, this dependency is seen as maturity and showing respect for the elders in the family. As extended families live under one roof in Asia, the elder of the family rules supreme. This custom is beginning to die out in large Asian cities. Because of apartment living, younger, more westernized and educated children move out on their own after they are financially able to afford the very expensive housing. In contrast, Western culture would characterize an adult child living in such a joint family as lacking initiative and ambition. Other than brief periods when young adults move back for economic reasons, a permanent joint living arrangement is seen in Western countries as one side "leeching off" the other.

We lived with my parents for about a year after our marriage, so my wife had a taste of living in a joint family. She was used to a similar atmosphere in her own parents' house, where her older brother and his wife also lived under one roof. There are very few "joint" families, defined as two or more adult generations living under one roof on a long-term basis, in the United States. However, advantages of such an arrangement include emotional support during difficult times, economies of scale with a reduction in living expenses, and security for the aging parents, who know that during illnesses they will have family to care for them. The grandchildren receive precious time with their grandparents who get the privilege of teaching those children about their origins, culture, language and religion.

I know two joint families in Ohio. In one instance, the married son invited his parents to build a home where they could all stay together. The daughter-in-law was a critical factor in allowing this arrangement to proceed. Her concordance allowed the husband's parents to be comfortable with the arrangement. At this writing the joint living arrangement is still new, and its long-term stability remains to be determined. The daughter-in-law probably agreed because her three children would have grandparents around them while growing up. The grandparents would be available to help with the children's activities.

The second household, with three generations under one roof, has been functioning much longer and been tested by the birth of triplets. In this instance, the bride came from India and was perfectly used to a joint family. Would this living arrangement work for most second generation children of immigrants? I doubt it. Elderly immigrants generally face disappointment when their expectations of their children taking care of them by living to-gether are not realized.

Life lessons: First generation immigrants, as well as their children, begin valuing their privacy and may find it hard to live in a joint family. If the opportunity arises to live in a multi-generation home, there are obvious ad-vantages but also sacrifices in sharing control. As a parent of a son, I would not even consider it unless my daughter-in-law was genuinely in favor of it for her family's benefit. Even then, I would find reasons not to do it. I would be concerned about upsetting the delicate parent-child-daughter-in-law bal-ance. If circumstances are such that joint living arrangements are possible, families must sit down together to make the best decision for all members.

THE ESSENTIALS

In no particular order, the core principles for most parents, immigrant or not, are: Love, trust, respect, pride and sharing the joy of being a family.

Love

Unconditional love between immigrant parents and their children can over-come any number of problems that the family will face. However much parental love is demonstrated and recognized by the children, conflicts will still arise and test this love. Therefore, it takes the nuts and bolts of trust and mutual respect to get the family through troubling times.

Trust

Trust takes a long time to develop, whether it is between parents and their children, at work among colleagues, or in any relationship. It only takes one poor decision in a moment to destroy trust. The basis of trust between family members is honesty, transparency, and consistency. Because any prior adverse experience colors our reactions, consistency is important. Children watch for consistency in their parents. If you are going to change the rules, you must ex-plain your reasons and the circumstances that justify the change in rules.

Respect

Respect is "consideration for someone or something of recognized worth."[2] There is a deep connection between trust and respect.[3] If you establish trust, respect follows. This is true of almost all relationships, not just with your children. If your children trust you as they are growing up, any positive or negative feedback becomes even more important to them. They will not suspect a hidden agenda for personal gain when you react negatively to any of their actions.

Pride

Taking pride in themselves, their abilities, and their heritage is part of making your children into confident human beings. Pride comes as a parent throws challenges at children and encourages them to accomplish the goals set for them. Goals that you set for the children must be achievable and meaningful.[4] That does not mean they have to be easy. The challenges may be "stretch goals," which may take sustained effort that goes beyond the norm. The challenges may create some anxiety and stress in the beginning, but achieving a goal undoubtedly leads to a great sense of accomplishment and pride. The goal may be an "A" in a subject, making the football team, or competing in a spelling bee.

Joy

Joy at being part of the family is the result of sustained effort by parents to create a culture of trust, respect, and pride in belonging to the family. Atchison points to the "tabula rasa" or blank sheet concept of translating values into behavior. This concept favors the nurture side over nature in determining the development of one's personality. Parents are the most important first responders in shaping a child's personality. They have the opportunity to influence not only the child's personality and future actions, but also their children's children and grandchildren!

Life lessons: Love, trust, respect, pride, and joy are all important in nurturing children. Children of immigrants are under unusual pressure and teeter between their parents' culture and the culture that surrounds them outside the home. A concentrated and sustained effort by parents to develop trust, respect, pride and joy at home will blunt these stresses.

RAISING THEM

Immigration is a traumatic event not only for the parents but the children as well. Depending on their age, immigrant children react differently. Parents must remember that they had a choice whether to immigrate or not. The children were involuntary immigrants. Some have called them "exiles."[5] The confusion is worse in adolescents, and much depends on how the parents are dealing with the loss of familiar surroundings. Immigrant parents, for the most part, bury their own concerns and hide their sadness and isolation in order to focus on making their children's lives better. They want to take care of their children as best they can. The question is, how much effort are they going to expend in putting their children first?

A lot of immigrants do not have immediate family around to assist with the children. Immigrants coming from higher socio-economic status are probably used to domestic help and may have never washed a dish. A fair number of immigrants do come with work experience, though. I know I had never cooked a meal, swept the carpet, or cleaned the bathroom. My wife had learned to cook a few months before our marriage but had never done any house cleaning either. All of a sudden, we were faced with everyday cleaning, cooking, and washing tasks with no servants around. These tasks consume a lot of time. We learned to be efficient with routine work at home so we could spend time with our children.

Time is the most valuable gift a parent can give to a child. Our daughter was born while I was an intern, and for the first two years of her life, I spent most of my waking hours working and missed seeing her each day until she was ready to go to bed. When I did come home, I longed for sleep. Sadly, those two years are a blur in my memory, other than that I remember what a beautiful baby my little girl was.

I tried to make up for this after this period in her life. During her lower, middle, and high school years, there were very few school events that I missed attending. Our medical practice group had instructed our office staff that, barring emergencies, our family commitments were to take priority over responsibilities to the practice. The other physicians would cover for the absent physician, and the favor would later be returned. This allowed the group, who shared common values, to truly participate in their children's lives. This enabled me to attend plays, soccer and tennis matches, gymnastic and dance recitals, parent-teacher meetings, and graduations. My wife declined to attend many parent teacher meetings, so I went to learn about my children.

We were fortunate that my highly educated wife decided to put her career on hold while our children were growing up. She gradually returned to part time studies as they attended school and finally, when they moved to college, she worked or studied full time.

I know the commonest advice for parents is to come together as a family for dinner every day. It is absolutely the ideal way to share the day with each other and catch up with what is happening at school and in the children's lives. However, if both parents are working and not coming home in a predictable fashion, you have to find alternate ways to share the day. Even if one parent has dinner with the children, the late arriving parent should try to get children at the table while he or she is finishing the meal.

Our situation may have been ideal, but most families used to two incomes will find it hard to have one parent at home with their children. That is a choice for a fair number of immigrant parents. Some immigrant women may not have worked before coming, and for them, the adaptation is easier. In contrast, for working women who marry and then immigrate with their husband, it can be a difficult time. Being alone at home with a baby or two, cooking, and cleaning, with no friends or family to share the day with, can be very depressing. I am sure it was hard for my wife. She was able to make the short-term sacrifice of her profession in order to see our children raised by a parent and not day care staff. Other immigrant couples may not be so lucky.

Life lessons: There is an obvious trade-off for parents in trying to go for that brass ring to ensure financial security for the family versus being there for children in their early years. There is no right answer that applies to everyone. Most immigrants want to teach their cultural or religious values to their children from the beginning. The absence of both parents makes this hard. If your occupation allows both of you to be there for the children you are rare. Most of us learn to trade, balance roles, feel guilty at times, and hope fervently that children turn into great human beings despite parental shortcomings.

LANGUAGE BARRIERS

The degree of difficulty in assimilating with a culture is related to the magnitude of differences between the motherland and the adopted country. Language, food, clothing, the media, the entertainment, and politics are all important variables that determine the difficulty of adjustment. Language and food are probably the factors that cause the most distress for immigrants.

According to the 2000 U.S. Census, 83 percent of the foreign born population speaks a language other than English at home and 51 percent speak English "less than very well." Those who speak Spanish primarily tend to speak English less fluently than Asian and Pacific Islanders. My family had an easier adjustment because my wife and I attended English-speaking Roman Catholic schools starting in kindergarten. People ask: "How come you do not have much of an accent?"

Learning to speak, understand, and write the English language can be hard for immigrants who have had little or no basic instruction. It may take multiple sources, such as radio, television, and classes to shed your shyness and feel comfortable with common expressions, idioms, and tenses. Speaking with an accent causes a lot of immigrants to hesitate in speaking English.

For my family, conversing in and teaching our children English was easy. In fact, our challenge was to help them become familiar with the two other languages we spoke at home. If you normally converse in your native language at home, it is worth taking classes to make sure you are familiar with what your children are learning. Similarly, considerable effort is required to teach your children your native language. Conversing with them usually elicits a response in English. Native language teaching has to start early before the children are embarrassed at their accent or do not want to speak in front of friends and family. It may mean deciding whether to drive children to the local native language church, temple, mosque, or Sikh Gurudwara worship center to have them learn to read and write the script. We started a little late and did not have, at the time, resources in town for teaching native languages to our children. By the time they were in their teens, it was too late. However, something about learning our language must have sunk in because both of them decided to take the time (on their own) in college to learn the language of their family heritage.

Food is another constant source of disagreement at home. It can also be a source of ridicule for immigrant children at school. If the food you pack for your child's lunch at school is different and particularly if it has spices with an ethnic odor, the food is going to be the source of unpleasant comments. One friend relates a way she dealt with the comments to her child. Her child was asked, "What garbage are you eating today?" She sat and explained to her child the nutritional value of the meal compared to the usual, refrigerated, pre-packed grocery store food other children carried to school. When the child's class was asked to share food items in class, the mother took the opportunity to make small snack sized potions. Once the other children tasted the food, they asked for her child to bring it in often.

Life lessons: If you want to teach children your native language, start early and be persistent. Be ready to answer the question "Why?" Most parents want their children to be able to communicate with grandparents and family members who do not speak the adopted language. Another reason may be that parents want their children to be able to read a religious text. The children's natural curiosity frequently will bring them back to learn more about their culture. Although you should stress the importance of learning the language, being hard nosed and creating a crisis is probably counter-productive.

PRIVACY VERSUS A PARENT'S RIGHT TO KNOW

The American concept of rugged individualism and a tendency to question authority is very different from most immigrants' native culture experience of identification with collective cooperation and obeisance to seniority. The shift from an extended family network to a nuclear family generates a lot of stress.[6] The family may either choose isolation, where members retreat into the family tradition, or disengagement with one another, where they go in different directions. Second-generation immigrants struggle between expectations of the parents' culture and that of their immediate surroundings.

When my wife and I were growing up, our friends were children of close relatives or friends who had been more or less screened and approved by our parents. Parents knew someone who knew someone else who knew your friend's family. When they did not have information they needed, they dug until they knew enough about our friends and their families. It was not unusual for parents to go through our things. Keeping secrets was hard, although we all did. In that culture, few things were private.

Children's privacy in the U.S. is valued to a ridiculous degree. How are we to keep an eye on our children? What is right and wrong in this culture? We are caught between two worlds. Do we spy on our children until we are confident of their direction? Parents have to decide how, when, and how much to watch over the affairs of their children. Since my children will be reading this, I am not about to incriminate myself with too much information on what their parents did to remain aware of what was happening in their lives.

A Spanish proverb puts it best: "Tell me who you are with and I will tell you who you are." When my children were young, they spoke to their friends. Nowadays, most children get their information from the Internet. How were we to know whether their friends were good influences? We rarely got to meet their parents, and when we did our meetings were brief and in formal surroundings. We eventually figured out ways to keep an eye on their friends. We encouraged our children to invite their friends to our house as much as possible for overnight stays or birthday parties. This way we could get to know them, or at least eye ball them.

I decide to join their music tastes. I grew up on pop music, and although it was hard to listen to Kenny Rogers after the Beatles and Elvis, I managed. My car radio was turned to popular music stations. I tried to read every news item that had to do with their favorite music or movie artists to see if I could scoop them on the latest news. I did so frequently and astonished them with some tidbit about Sting or Michael Jackson, or Annie Lenox. I took my children to several concerts, including Michael Jackson in drizzly Cleveland Stadium, Sting at multiple locations, the Pointer Sisters, In Living Color, Kool and the

Gang, and others. My children did not always want to sit together. I didn't blame them.

We went to see In Living Color at Newport Hall, a rundown place on High Street in Columbus, Ohio. I knew the group was going to be loud. To protect my ears I borrowed large, red, over-the-ear hunting muffs that I took in a paper bag. As soon as the lights went down I put them on. The kids decided they did not want to be seen with some older guy with red ear protectors! I understood. I drove my daughter and six of her best friends in our van to Blossom Center near Akron to see a shirtless Sting for the umpteenth time. She still remembers it and tells her friends about my patience in putting up with seven estrogen laden teenagers and staying the night at my brother's house. I often joked that she might as well write Sting and Trudy (his wife) a big check including her trust fund instead of buying every record, tape, t-shirt, and brochure at concerts.

These actions established a relationship built upon shared experiences, including music. This relationship enabled me to get to know my children's friends and be comfortable with them. Their friends said I was quite "cool." What I did not explain was that my object was not to appear cool but to spend time with them and get to know the company they were keeping. When they were older, I was not comfortable with some of my children's friends, but at that stage the children were driving, and there was little I could do besides trying my best to get information. You know how that went down.

Nowadays, the need for parents to be vigilant is even more urgent. If I were a parent of teenagers today, I would be alarmed by the deterioration of our youth. A biennial national survey of 12,474 high school students by the Josephson Institute, called "The 2002 Josephson Institute Report Card on the Ethics of American Youth," showed that 74 percent of students admitting to cheating on an exam at least once in the past year compared to 61 percent in 1992.[7] The number of students who stole something from a store went from 31 percent to 38 percent in one year. The percentage who admitted to lying to their teachers and parents increased significantly (68 percent in 1992 to 78 percent in 2002).

It gets worse. The National Institute on Drug Abuse and the University of Michigan found in a study of adolescent behavior that 19 percent of eighth graders and 47 percent of twelfth graders admitted to using illegal drugs.[8]

The incidence of teen pregnancies makes a parent who has a young daughter at home cringe. According to UNICEF, the U.S. teenage birth rate of 52.1 births per 1,000 women aged fifteen to nineteen is first among twenty-nine countries.[9] Four of every ten births in the U.S. are to unwed mothers. These are all our kids that are in trouble.

So, what is more important to you, your child's hurt feelings from having his or her privacy invaded or their safety and health? A common parenting mistake is to try to win a child's favor by letting them have their way when you know that there are risks involved. Appearing to be "hip" in front of their friends gets you points. Boasting to your fellow immigrant parents of not being allowed into your son's room may make you look like a trusting parent. However, we are not their friends until they are mature adults capable of making logical and well-thought-out decisions. I am not saying adults do not make mistakes. Of, course we do. The point is that we have to hold their hands till we feel they have developed the critical thinking skills that allow them to make rational decisions that take them closer to the goals they set for themselves.

Curfew hours are a common source of conflict in most homes, but particularly in immigrant families. Immigrant parents usually had very little input into their own time when they were growing up. They absolutely had to be home on school nights or weekends. When our children were in high school, we set 9 p.m. as curfew time during school nights and 11 p.m. during weekends. Sunday evening was treated as a weekday and Friday evening as a weekend night. In the rare case when they were running late, they were required to call us personally and explain the reason for being late.

It is a good idea to stay up until teens arrive home. A close friend had a brilliant policy that applied even when their children were in college. One of them stayed up until the children came home, and then the child was required to give them a good night hug before going to bed. This way they could use their sense of smell to detect any odor of smoke or alcohol. Curfew hours can be relaxed as children grow up and become more responsible. Until then it is necessary to hold firm despite a multitude of excuses.

The progress of the relationship from parent to friend is a slow and tortuous process with twists and turns. You think they are there, give them some slack and bang! A bad decision is made, and they are back in the doghouse. Granted, some children never make what you consider to be adult decisions, but at some point you have to cut them loose. My father was very strict until a late stage in my life because I was living at home, as was customary in our culture. However, once he saw that I had not broken his trust, the rope was not just slackened but totally thrown away. Each child is different. Some require a very gradual slackening of the marionette strings by the manipulator or adult controlling the child's actions. Other children are ready to be left alone once they pass a few critical test situations that come up as a matter of course. Above all, monitor your child till they show you that they are responsible enough to make mature decisions. Love them but be firm.

Life lessons: The parental role as the authoritarian figure or a friend is not cast in stone. It changes at various stages in the child's life. The best outcome is when you are sharing their good times and their disappointments with them, and you see yourself as a supporting cast in a play where they are the main character. A supporting cast member does not usurp the role played by the main actor, and yet the star of the show needs the supporting cast to succeed. Know when to be in the background and when to take over if the script is not being followed. Privacy is important, but if you suspect deviation from important principles you have laid down, you have the right to break the rules. You just cannot get caught doing it. Parents are parents first and friends second. There will be time later for friendship.

PEER PRESSURE

A universal struggle for children is how to deal with peer pressure. Children of immigrants are not only exposed to peer pressure but are forced in some ways to "disown" parts of their own way of life. It may be in matters of food, clothing, music, or articles of faith. Examples include the wearing of a hijab for Muslim girls, a turban for Sikh boys, or a prayer thread around the wrist for Hindu children.

Children may be greatly conflicted if what they see practiced at home is denigrated as "weird" by the American teen culture or if they are made to feel inferior for the same reason. Asian children from culturally conservative families will often feel awkward and reticent about wearing shorts at sporting events, wearing bathing suits, or being nude in communal showers or locker rooms. Add to this the outwardly distinct clothing or symbols of their religion and the children are almost being asked to pick a side. If they do not understand the meaning and significance of these practices, they cannot justify them at school or to their friends. They are left with no choice but to separate from their family culture. They may join in the insults. Until they grow up, they need to be proud of their culture, and it is the job of the parents to rationally explain the reasons for practicing some distinct aspects of their culture.

Peer pressure can prove to be a good thing, or it can be a bad influence for children. How can they stay true to their own values and principles yet not alienate friends with whom they may disagree? They may be pressured to conform to the practices of a group that participates in activities their parents have advised them against. Yet, if they decline to participate, they are labeled as "sissies" or uncool.

It is the duty of parents to help children select good friends who will exert a positive influence on them. Parents have to teach children that best friends do not necessarily like the same things. Just listening to them express their fears and insecurities is often all that is needed. Most times they are not looking for parental advice, but rather for someone who listens without passing judgment or jumping in with advice. The more you talk to them, the more likely it is that they will let you meet their friends. It is important to allow your children some room to experiment. It is more important to discern whether their friends are solid individuals who are putting effort into their school work.

Clothes are a very frequent source of disagreement in any house, but clothing styles can particularly be a source of contention among two generations of immigrants. Cultures vary on the degree to which body parts are exposed in public. For some immigrants, tight clothing, shorts, revealing tops, and bikinis are too permissive, or even obscene. Muslim women may be uncomfortable without a hijab or a chador covering their heads. Hindu women feel exposed without a dupatta (a thin piece of clothing draped over their shoulders covering their upper torso) or a sari that covers the body. Children want to wear what they see their friends wearing and what their favorite television actors have on. I am talking just about the type of clothing and not so much the brand name that may appear on clothing and shoes.

Sometimes *modesty* is not a word in the clothing style vocabulary. It is not unheard of for children to leave home properly covered up and take off a layer or two by the time they reach school or their friend's home. Of course, there is no problem if the clothes do not hide anything, but, most immigrants dress conservatively, meaning not a lot of skin is showing.

The fiat, "Don't wear that because I say so" lasts only while they are still young and not influenced by friends, television, or the movies. A lot of parents make the argument based on their religion or culture. It is less prudent to simply impose your will than to convince children that they do not have to dress like models or Hollywood stars to be liked or respected. Try to let their personality make the case.

Life lessons: Peer pressure is insidious and gradually seeps into every facet of children's lives. Constant communication and occasionally giving in to small demands, within reason, is a good way to handle peer pressure instead of constantly saying no and risking interrupting the parent-child dialogue.

GENDER ROLES: RESPECT FOR MOM

There is a contradiction in the way women are treated in Eastern culture. Women are exalted as goddesses, and children are instructed that if someone wants to get a shortcut to heaven, all they have to do is look under their mother's feet. The implication is that to serve your mother and lie at her feet will get you a pass into heaven. Hindu scriptures and history are replete with women of strength who can serve as role models.

The list starts with Sita, wife of Lord Rama, who is considered a model of the perfect woman and the heroine of the *Ramayana*, one of the most holy books for Hindus. Then, in the epic *Mahabharata*, we have Kunti, the mother of the five Pandva brothers, whose faith in Lord Krishna was absolute.

There is Draupadi, the wife of all five Pandvas, whose insults in the court resulted in a war that led to many millions of deaths. Her independence and strong will are admired. Mirabai (1498-1547) is also a devotee of Lord Krishna. Her decision not to commit sati (self immolation when her husband died) led to her persecution. She is considered one of the foremost saints in history, and her poems are still recited widely. More recently, there is Queen Jhansi (1828-1858) who became a symbol of bravery and resistance to British rule in India. These are but a few well-known examples of strong and well-respected women role models in the history of the Indian sub-continent.

On the other hand, the culture is strongly paternalistic, and women are mostly subservient to men. Things are changing rapidly, particularly with increasing opportunities for education and economic independence. My family is traditional in the sense that my wife put her professional ambitions on hold while she raised our two children. I was busy with my surgical residency, and a two-career household would have been a confusing place for children already stressed by the pull of two very different cultures. We never actually discussed the option of her working and my staying home for several reasons. She had a college degree from outside the United States, and I was likely to end up in a reasonably predictable job. It was assumed that she would be the one to put her career on hold.

We were unaware of our own overt or covert behavior concerning gender roles. This affected our son. He saw his dad bringing home the money and becoming known in the community. I saw some disrespect in the way he talked to his mother, and I jumped on the issue quickly. Most full time mothers get tired of being the nurturer and the disciplinarian and use a common threat: "Wait until your father comes home." Another threat is "Don't do it again, or I will tell dad." But when a line is crossed in the case of boys, it is judicious to take action quickly. I had a couple of those sit-down dad-to-son talks. The explanation was simple: "Your mother is a lot smarter than your dad. She is the only one in the family with a gold medal in the entire university for academic performance. The only reason she is not at work is you, so you'd better treat her with respect or else. This behavior will not be tolerated."

IT WORKED

I have been lucky to have fairly strong women in my life. My mother is definitely subservient to my father, but she is also strong in her own way and knows how to push the right buttons and when to take a stand. My wife has a spine of steel that is hidden and covered with sweetness and a smile.

The value of father's being involved in a positive way has been confirmed by extensive research. Both partners can impede the father's contribution to the development of the child by "gatekeeping." Gatekeeping is negative feedback. A mother can, by negative feedback, discourage fathers from being closely involved with feeding, changing, and playing with the baby all the way to participating in school functions. Fathers can similarly disappear into the shadows or be too passive in bringing up children. These actions can generate tension and disagreements that play out in front of the children.

We decided early in our marriage to keep our disagreements private and not argue our points of view in front of the children. We succeeded for the most part. As it turns out, probably too much. As recently as seven years ago, my wife and I had a somewhat heated argument in the company of both of our children. There was a shocked look on their faces. Later, they remarked that this was the first time they had seen us argue. While growing up, they had assumed that couples do not argue at all. This had left them confused, since what they saw at home conflicted with what they observed elsewhere and in the popular media.

Life lessons: The socialization of children in regard to gender roles in most families occurs in an "informal" fashion. Children learn behaviors by observation rather than formal education. Although both sexes need to be watched, fathers need to take decisive steps to stop any behavior (particularly by their male children) that in any way belittles the stay-at-home mother. If tolerated with a "wink and a nod" this may carry over into their future relationships with women. It goes without saying that any verbal abuse towards women in the house is a harbinger of misogynistic behavior later in life.

PUBLIC DISPLAY OF AFFECTION

There are differences between cultures pertaining to displays of affection shown between family members. Immigrant families, in general, do not hold hands, kiss, or hug in public. On the one hand, kissing between men and women in public is considered vulgar by most people. For example, in the busiest film industry in the world (India's) no kissing scenes have been allowed by the censor board until recently. On the other hand, the concept of one's own space is foreign to South Asians. People live together in much smaller spaces, often several people to a room, and they do not feel uncomfortable with sharing beds, clothes, shoes, and dishes. In Western culture, the thought of having to share a bed or personal items is not pleasant and to be avoided if possible. Although, there are physicians in the U.S. who are also uncomfortable with physical contact, by and large, elderly patients like the healing touch.

Cultural norms simply differ. I grew up seeing almost no outward display of affection between my parents. That did not mean I did not know that there was a strong bond between them. When I immigrated to the U.S., the difference was striking. Parents would hug and kiss their children, couples would hold hands and kiss each other on the street, and friends would hug at the slightest excuse. I heard couples tell each other, "I love you" in public. I was truly puzzled the first time I heard guests banging their spoons on their wine glasses at a wedding reception, taunting the couple to kiss each other. It took a few years, but I changed. I am still somewhat reserved, and my wife and I never exhibit any sign of affection in public. However, we both hugged and kissed our children as they grew up, and I believe this has strengthened our bond with them. I have seen new immigrant's exhibit affection on the streets that I am sure they would not show in their native countries.

Life lessons: For immigrants the advice is to try and adopt some of the Western cultural habits with a liberal dose of affection on display in front of children. It becomes a little awkward during their teen years, but as they grow up, you will be able to pick up where you left off.

HOW MUCH FREEDOM?

Few immigrant parents have a background in child psychology or have taken extensive educational courses on how to raise children. Most parents read a few pop psychology paperbacks and then wonder if all the conflicting opinions actually apply to them. A lot of issues for immigrant parents are the same as for any other parents in the U.S., except that the anxiety is much more heightened.

To some degree all parents learn to fly by the seat of their pants. Sometimes we come off looking very smart, and at other times we feel we are incapable of handling these aliens in our homes. For example, the hardest parenting issue during the teen years is deciding when they are ready for things such as staying out late, viewing adult movies, driving by themselves, spending the night with their best friends, or dating. In short, the answer is that there is no hard and fast rule. It depends on the maturity of the child, the trust you have established with them and how successfully you have managed to brainwash them with your principles.

For instance, I felt our son was ready to drive by himself shortly after he turned sixteen. However, I wanted reassurance that he was going to follow the rules. I sat down with him and had him put his signature on an index card with his promises to obey curfew hours, not to have alcohol or allow any passengers in the car with alcohol on them, and to call home if he was going to be late by more than fifteen minutes. His sister witnessed and signed the deal. I never had to pull the card out of my desk drawer for a violation. He knew what the rules were ahead of time and that I was serious about his compliance with them.

You, as a parent, may have to relearn everything you once knew about dating, if you even dated at all. Your children will be regarded as strange if they are not seeing someone in high school.

Immigrants wrestle with their principles. They need to be able to deal with children who are growing up in a Western culture. That culture allows teenagers the freedom to make choices they would not be able to make in other countries. Some talk about sending their children back to their native country during the teen years so that they grow up with the same rules of the game that parents played under. Some actually have followed through on this threat. Others simply accept the new culture's-American rules and go with the flow.

The vast majority, however, are in constant conflict with their children and with each other during this vulnerable period in their children's lives. This conflict almost always starts out with being on the telephone and who is at the other end.

"Whose house are you going to?"

"Who else is going to meet you at the mall?"

"Are there going to be boys (or girls) there with you?"

"You are NOT going to watch THAT show."

"You are too young to go out alone."

Parents argue among themselves about who is going to have the talk about the "birds and the bees!" We faced all of the above hurdles. Some we glided over with ease; some we struggled with, and others we simply went around. What seemed like a major crisis at the time simply did not turn out to be that serious. I know of several instances in which children started dating someone in high school who the parents did not care for at all. All attempts at convincing the children about the character of the object of their affection were of no avail. Usually, children find out the truth and start trusting their parent's first impression, but not always.

We have not seen the need to say, "We told you so" very many times.

The question for most parents is not, "Do we allow him/her to date?" The real question is how you are going to get enough information about their intended love interest without sparking a revolution. Unless you are an ultra-conservative person who does not want to allow any one-to-one contact between the sexes, the question again is not whether to allow dating, but when, at what speed, and not so much with whom.

The trick is to stay in the loop when the child is thinking about these decisions. My father was an extremely strict disciplinarian and gradually eased up on the restrictions I had. But when he did ease up, it was very swift, and I went from chafing under the rules one day to almost total freedom to fly at warp speed the next.

Our children grew up before the explosion of the Internet. Exposure to certain programs on television was problematic. The first time I saw something really vulgar on Music Television (MTV), I almost flipped. We banned MTV for over six months, until it became obvious that our daughter was watching at her friend's place. The general themes of 'anything goes," material greed, minimal clothing, and sexually suggestive programs were anathema to us, but to totally ban television in the house appeared to be unrealistic. Possibly, we could have done this but we were not willing to pay the price in terms of harmony within our family.

Life lessons: Children need discipline that does not arrive and depart like a sudden gust of wind. Consistency is the watchword here. It is confusing to the child when your standard is very demanding one day and then permissive another day. Parenting is like flying a kite. If you have ever flown a kite (patang) in the contests in which kite battles kite, each is flown with a string (Dor) that has been treated with a mixture of a special glue and ground glass (manja). The objective is to trap and then cut an opponent's kite string. Freedom is given with strings attached till an adult decides they are ready to be cut loose and fly on their own. While you are flying the kite though, glass-encrusted kite strings sure can cause finger skin cuts as you maneuver, just as too much freedom can cause painful incidents. Controlling the pace of allowing privileges is emotionally painful for parents. No two parents are going to agree on actions that reach levels at which disciplinary measures are called for. However, this disagreement must be in private. If some delay is necessary so you can put your heads together and get a consensus, then that is what you need to do.

BEING THERE AND LISTENING

One of the best ways to persuade others is with your ears—by listening to them, according to Dean Rusk, who was U.S. secretary of state from 1961 to 1969 under presidents John Kennedy and Lyndon Johnson.

Parenting often involves quietly sacrificing without the children being remotely aware of your needs. They are in a world of their own. As an adult, you are able to see the trees in the forest and remember that their needs take precedence over your needs. If you cannot sacrifice, better not have children. The hard part is that when you do bring up all the things you gave up or went without so they could have what you never did, some children may retort that parents are expected to sacrifice. Maybe so. If you do not want to hear their response to your attempt to make them feel guilty, you are advised not to make this argument at all.

More than anything else parents do for their children, it is paramount that they are at hand when needed. I remember how guilty we felt when we took a few days off for a vacation without our children. We called the elderly nanny who lived with our children for a few days to check in. She told us that our son's pet hamster had died. He was about ten years old and was really upset. He wanted us there. She finally convinced him to go in the woods and bury the hamster without us. I doubt we missed anything of significance after this. Problems may seem trivial, but at a young age each problem is earth shattering. Children may want to share and seek advice. Sometimes they don't necessarily want to talk and tell you what their problem is. They just want to have you around while they process the issues.

As I said above, trust is very valuable currency within the family. Trust comes from truly listening. One of my many shortcomings is that I sometimes do not have the patience to listen. A surgeon's personality is focused on the end-result and getting to the point. Many times, I have had to bite my tongue when listening to my daughter relating an episode blow by blow, punctuated by "and then," followed by "so, then." I feel like saying, "So, what happened." To my regret, I sometimes do. Or I have been guilty of using conversation chillers like "I know that" or "You told me that before." Interrupting or suggesting words before the person you are talking to is finished speaking or even finishing a sentence for him or her is another way to discourage conversation.

Non-verbal cues are probably just as important. I have been caught typing, reading the newspaper or watching television while someone has attempted to talk to me. Learn from me. Stop that. Make eye contact and keep it there.

Atchison points out that there are three types of listening: Selective listening (hearing and reacting), active listening (engaging and focusing), and reflective listening (accepting and supporting). Selective listening is what most of us (including me) practice. We carefully listen with the idea of finding favorable or unfavorable points and then providing a solution, assuming that the child wants our feedback.

Active listening implies a more pro-active approach, in which the parent is more engaged. Non-directive maneuvers are used, such as asking questions and para-phrasing the child's statements. If the child is describing a conflict with a friend who talked about her behind her back, you might respond with, "So, you are saying that she went and talked behind your back?" This validation of her complaint may lead to a solution. My tendency has been to try to come up with a quick fix to the problem being described and give my child the benefit of my experience. In a lot of instances, that is not what the child is looking for.

Reflective listening involves accepting her complaint, providing support and in most cases letting her come up with a solution. My wife and I are both guilty of responding with the least supportive response by suggesting at some point in the conversation that the offended person should "get over it." That is a losing proposition that may erode the trust you have built up between you and your child. True, the child will get over it in time, but that statement does not help at all. An empathic response does not mean you want to be an enabler or encouraging co-dependency.[10]

After you have expressed empathy, you can gradually steer the conversation to active listening and an attempt to have the child come up with a solution to her friend's bad behavior. Children will remember when you were there for them and when you were not listening. Sometimes it is the small events that stick in their memory.

The thousands of events that make up our lives are like grains of sand that pass quickly through a sand clock. Major and minor events should be looked upon as opportunities to be captured as precious moments in your children's lives. Just imagine that your children's eyes are a camera, and they are clicking away. Many years later they will look at the pictures and remember how much attention you were paying to them.

On the subject of cameras, our memories are captured in numerous pictures and videos over the years. We collected many photographic memories of our parents and grandparents. When our children were in their mid-twenties, all of the pictures and videos were converted into digital formats. The DVD copies were handed over to them so they could pass them on to their children. In addition, special moments such as high school graduations or noteworthy birthdays, such as the sixteenth birthday, should be celebrated with an eye to the future. For some of these events, you should be thinking," What should I do to make this event standout as a memory?"

I will give you an example. When our son was turning sixteen, my wife and I debated what would really surprise him. He thought of us as extremely strait-laced, fairly serious, conservative, family-oriented people. So, what would shock him and make him remember his sixteenth birthday forever? His older sister and close friends were at our home to celebrate with a cake. The doorbell rang and in walked a belly dancer. This was a major shock for him and his friends. She did the usual shaking and shimmying her chest and her rear end in his face while he was trying to hide and ignore his friends, who were dying of laughter. He remembers that day like it was yesterday, and every time it comes up, he remarks on how we embarrassed him. Under that exterior, I am sure he associates that act with love and fondness because he knows we had to get over our considerable inhibitions to allow what happened to occur.

Life lessons: It really takes a lot of effort for parents to drop everything and listen to children talk about some trivial thing that happened at school. But, you must. Think of their brain as a super powerful camera. The camera is constantly clicking and taking micro-pictures of your inter-actions with them throughout their childhood These are stored in the large hard drive that is their cerebral cortex. How do want them to remember you?

CONFLICT AND DISAGREEMENTS

Cooperation and conflict are the yin and yang of dealing with children. Raising children is a constant series of negotiations. It makes little sense to try to win every battle. Naturally, a parental perspective is very different from a child's viewpoint. You think you are wiser with your past experiences, while the child is convinced that what may have worked in the home country simply will not work now. You are both dug in and spinning your wheels getting yourself deeper in a rut. You may think you have won at the time, but if your child sees the negotiations as inequitable, you will have lost.

Try not to start with an entrenched position. That does not mean you should not have a strong point of view. It means that you do not present the view as inflexible without regard for your child's view. In some cases, as the adult, you have already decided the right course of action, but you should hear the other side out as a measure of respect. Give your reasons first, and then present the solutions if the problem demands one.

The movie *The Namesake*[11] depicts children of immigrants rebelling against their parents' efforts to bring them up with a strong dose of their native culture. The Ganguli couple is "FOB" ("fresh off the boat") immigrants to Boston from the state of Bengal in India in the late 1960s. Their son is born in Boston and is named Gogol when the selection by grandparents of his name does not make it in time from India. In our culture, the child's name is generated by a pundit or holy priest. The priest, after a prayer session, indicates the first letter of the newborn's name and suggests several names starting with that letter. The grandparents have a big role to play along with the parents.

Gogol tries hard to live the typical American life. He loathes and is cynical when his parents continue to cling to their Bengali roots and try (unsuccessfully) to initiate their son into the culture.

The Gangulis' life story is that of a lot of immigrants in the United States, who strive to bring their up their children with their traditions. Gogol is shown struggling through self-discovery and initially rejects his parent's values until he comes to understand his parents' sacrifices and his own need for his culture.

The struggle between the two generations of immigrants is fairly typical. This conflict usually manifests itself, whether dealing with name, clothing, food, taste in music, friends, religion, or respect for family members.

As the children are trying to find themselves and sort out the balance between their immigrant roots and their land of birth, their first impulse is to reject the old and identify with the new and their friends. Maira calls this the second migration, when young adults decide to emotionally return to their ancestry in a general sense.[12]

Despite our best efforts to have our children mix with the children of our friends, most of their friends were non-Asians. Like most immigrants, we tried to teach our children our customs and to learn to speak our native language. We succeeded to some degree, but it took time. Parents tend to think that what we repeat over and over is going through one ear and out the other ear. It does not appear to be having any effect. To the contrary, most of what you repeat is captured, stored, and processed inside the brain, to be acted on later.

It is akin to seeding your lawn in a less than ideal season. Some of the seeds do germinate over time. Both of our children, without any prodding or coercion, took Hindi language classes in college. One took a six-week summer session, and the other took two grammar courses in college. They understand the two languages we speak and can converse when necessary. It would have been a mistake to force the issue when they were in their teen years. They are both as well versed in our culture, history, religion, and customs as anyone and they make us proud.

Despite your best efforts, disagreements will arise. Sometimes it is just a matter of opinion or taste and of no great consequence. In these cases it is better to give in. Downsizing the conflict by agreeing to discuss an issue further and allowing your child to save face may create some positive momentum. At times children are simply trying to test your tolerance of actions that are not necessarily bad but are outside of the informal rules set for the family. Our son came to me during his middle school years to ask what my reaction would be if he decided to have earrings. This was at a time when earrings were just becoming the rage. Kids were having their ears pierced and their hair colored, but the craze had not yet progressed to body decorations on tongues, belly buttons and other sundry places. My son was very surprised when I said, "Sure! You can have earrings or purple hair if you like, as long as you study and bring home the grades."

Take a stand on something that really matters. What does it matter if children color their hair red or have a small tattoo, as long as it is safely and tastefully done? The earring issue was a small one to give on, and I wanted him to understand what was really important. In the end, he was too straight laced to have his ears pierced!

Other disagreements can be serious, with consequences that matter. As a parent you have the maturity to see beyond that day, week, or month. In those circumstances, exercise parental authority to make sure your child listens and follows your decision. By and large, these decisions can be talked out and explained. Sometimes, the child still does not agree. Then you just have to enforce the decision.

Life lessons: The principles you lay down for your children to follow should be like an aerial view shown on Google earth with the street view zoomed out of the picture. Try not to get into arguments over small issues, but constantly emphasize the big picture.

NOTES

1. G. R. Sodowsky and J. C. Carey, "Asian Indian Immigrants in America: Factors Related to Adjustment," *Journal of Multicultural Counseling and Development* 15.3 (1957): 129-141.

2. Scott Foresman, *Advanced Dictionary* (Upper Saddle River, NJ: Pearson Education, 1997): "Respect."

3. Thomas A. Atchison, *Leadership's Deeper Dimensions* (Chicago, IL: Health Administration, 2006), 25.

4. Ibid.

5. Leon Grinberg and Rebeca Grinberg, *Psychoanalytic Perspectives on Migration and Exile*, trans. N. Festinger (NewHaven, CT: Yale University Press. 1989), 125.

6. J. Landau, "Therapy with Families in Cultural Transition," in *Ethnicity and Family Therapy*, ed. M. McGoldrick, J. K. Pearce, and J. Giordano (New York: Guilford, 1982), 552-572.

7. "The Ethics of American Youth: 2002," Josephson Institute Report Card, http://www.charactercounts.org/programs/reportcard/2002/index.html.

8. National Institute on Drug Abuse, National Institutes of Health, http://www.drugabuse.gov/drugpages/MTF.HTML.

9. "American People Stats, NationMaster.com, http://www.nationmaster.com/country/us-united-states/peo-people. See also "The Ethics of American Youth: 2002," Josephson Institute Report Card, http://www.charactercounts.org/programs/report-card/2002/index.html.

10. Atchison, *Leadership's Deeper Dimensions*, 25.

11. Fox Searchlight Pictures, 2006.

12. S. Maira, "Making Room for a Hybrid Space: Reconsidering Second Generation Ethnic Identity," *Sanskriti*, 6.6 (1995), at http://www.proxsa.org/resources/sanskriti/dec95/sunaina.html.

Chapter Three

Values

Values are defined as "beliefs of a person or social group in which they have an emotional investment"[1] or "an individual's accepted standards of right or wrong."[2] Values are internal convictions and beliefs that drive our behavior and guide our major decisions.[3]

Values are necessarily subjective and depend somewhat on the culture surrounding the person who is attempting to explain them for his or her own personal reference. Therefore, even if two people from the same culture agree on the broad outline of a values system, they may not necessarily agree on the details. Two people from entirely different cultures in diametrically opposite corners of the earth may have similar values.

How did you come up with your set of values? It is not likely that your parents specifically sat you down and enumerated them or had you write them down. Nevertheless, you accumulated a set of experiences over time, deciding what was right or wrong. You now wish to teach your values to your children.

Your children will pick up on the values you demonstrate on a daily basis. To them, it is not important whether these values came with you or were adopted after you came to the United States. Values may or may not be specific to your culture or language. Your values will, however, influence what you plan to accomplish during your life.

Looking back at our lives is a favorite pastime for most of us. I also wish I had done some things differently. Most of all, I wish I had put down on paper the things that I valued most and how I wanted to live my life. Oh, I thought about it like everyone else, but I did not bother to write my values down and examine then frequently so I could prioritize things. It takes some time to set your own priorities in life. It was not until after I had finished my surgical residency training and was thirty years old that I had a chance to think about what was important. I had no time during my internship and residency to think about anything other than sleeping when I came home after being on call.

Some people have a tentative mental list of things they would like to accomplish during their lives, based upon things that really matter to them. I have always maintained that people, at some point, should write their own mission statements. Like most people, my mission statement was in my head but never written down on paper. When I started part-time MBA classes, one of the exercises in an early course forced me to focus further on my personal mission and vision in order to put it down on paper. That was important. A written document is hard to dismiss.

The mission statement should be a clear representation of the individual's purpose for existing. The misconception is that this type of exercise is for the business or academic person. Wrong. Paul Beeston states:

> To live your mission is the most generous thing you can do. Your mission is always going to make a major contribution to your life, the lives of others and the planet. Humankind and the planet need you to live your mission. Your mission is part of the tapestry of life and without it there are stitches missing. Is there anything more important for you to do?[4]

To simplify the process of writing a mission statement, you should ask yourself the questions "What do I care about the most?" "Who do I care about?" and "What do I want to accomplish and why?"

Based upon answers to these questions, I wrote this mission statement:

- To remember my Creator at all times, and know that I will have to answer for all my actions and deeds in this life.
  To recognize that my potential for personal growth is infinite.
- To lead my life so my family can remember me as an honest human being, who was trustworthy in marriage, [and who] cared for them deeply and left a legacy of love and core values to be passed on.
- I will value loyalty, treat friends and co-workers with dignity, be tolerant, and strive to remain humble.
- To be a model of professional integrity and have my patients say that I cared.
- To try and maintain a sense of humor, know that perpetual happiness in life was not guaranteed at birth, and remember that the bad days shall pass.

When your children are young, it may be a little premature to ask them to write a mission statement. However, it is not too early to prod them into thinking about issues more important than the next sleep over. As they get older, try to get them to express what is important to them and why. Certainly, by the time they are juniors in high school if not sooner, the values you have taught them should be transparent. This is the time to guide them in the process of writing their mission statement. The statement can be revised as they grow up and have a chance to further dwell on issues important to them.

Life lessons: Everyone needs a roadmap to get from here to there. Encourage your children at some point in their high school years to think about and work on their mission statement. Call it something else if you think the phrase "mission statement" is too wonkish. They can modify it as time goes on and as they learn more about themselves. The statement gives them something to focus on when multiple goals vie for their attention.

VALUES AND ETHICS

Most of us do not think much about our own values until someone like a child questions the ethics around those values. It may be as simple as keeping extra change from a grocery clerk or fibbing about your age to get in at a discounted rate in a movie. Children will notice these things and at some point will throw them in your face when you start to lecture them about morality and values. If there is a gap between what you tell them and what they see you do, you can be sure it will come up later. If you have a double standard because the standard you set for your children and what you practice is different, it will be noticed.

I am not saying that all of us are so perfectly consistent that this should never happen. But, it helps to think things through ahead of time and realize that your actions are subject to review by your children.

Life Lessons: Keep it simple. It's the small incidents that add up to make an impression on your children. While the children will see your imperfections, you need to show them how you practice your values. Two-facedness will absolutely kill any big speeches you may give them about being ethical.

BEHAVIOR AND DISCIPLINE

Understanding behavior and the reward system you choose in your family has a lot to do with disciplinary actions that may be necessary. Atchison remarks that behavior is different from feelings, attitudes, and emotions. Behavior is observable and objective, while feelings, attitudes, and emotions are subjective.[5] He assigns three separate characteristics to behavior: It is observable, measurable, and repeatable.

For example, if your child is always late for events, the action is observable, measurable, and repeatable. It also is undesirable behavior that can and should be altered. However, you may assign a motive to his action of being late for a specific event and verbalize that he does not care about the significance of the event. What Atchison is pointing out is that the latter, isolated, action is not appropriate for punishment. He suggests that behavioral specificity and objectivity should be used in determining reward or punishment, rather than subjectivity. In addition, recognition of a child by a parent is not necessarily contingent on a particular set of actions. A reward, in contrast, whether monetary or otherwise, is given because the child has achieved or exceeded expectations. Both can be used, depending on the circumstances. After trying various recognition and reward systems, most parents come to realize that you can catch more flies with honey than vinegar.

I only got spanked twice as a child. Once, when I was six or seven years old, I asked for some money to get candy cigarettes. My grandmother and dada (my father) were sitting in the jhoola. A "jhoola" is a large swing mounted on four strong legs that are anchored to the floor. Several people can sit for relaxation on a jhoola. In those days, a person was hired to pull the large swing to keep it in motion. My grandmother said "Come here and get it from me." I walked over to her and took the money from her hands. My father then called me over, slapped me, and told me that I should not have taken the money from her. I peed in my shorts. I never asked anyone else for money again.

The second time was when I was around eight years old and was called on to assist my brother, who was unsuccessfully trying to light a fire in the garage. Unfortunately, the car was still parked in the garage! He had failed to light a fire and I was showing him how it was done. He got caught, as he usually did, and promptly blamed me for showing him how to start a fire. I again received one slap, except this time I didn't pee in my shorts. What really turned me off corporal punishment, however, was my experience at a boarding school. At age ten, I was punished once in class for not having done my homework. Father Trinidad the principal, who later reminded me of the Hulk on the television program, called me to his office and gave me a choice of taking it on the behind or the hands. I chose both hands. The stiff stick came down hard. My hands were numb for hours. I cried and never forgot my homework again.

This early experience turned me against corporal punishment. There are clear differences in how most immigrants from non-Western countries would define domestic violence or child abuse. In general, this is seen as an issue for the family to resolve rather than social services or some other governmental agency. Although not perfect, the U.S. has laws to address perpetrators against women and children that are much more muscular than in most other parts of the world.

We have been fortunate that our children hardly ever gave us cause to worry too much, other than the usual teenage shenanigans. Yes, we occasionally made up rules as we went, improvising as most parents do, and using our instincts. We tried to set clear boundaries ahead of time. When our son reached driving age, the rules were put in writing. We discussed and agreed on rules that were not to be violated. His sister witnessed and signed the index card. I never had to pull the rules card out to confront him or enforce the consequences of breaking the rules by taking away driving privileges. Our son and daughter learned about self-reliance, discipline, setting priorities, and dealing with adversity. Those are lessons worth teaching children at an early age.

I do not believe in repeated reminders to children such responsibilities as doing homework or returning home on time within curfew hours. You have to be loving but firm and lay out consequences for not meeting certain standards. If you have to raise your voice to get your children to pay attention, you have probably lost the battle. No matter what the punishment is for a given violation of house rules, children should always know, without a shred of doubt, that they are loved. Love should be clearly separated from consequences of action or inaction.

Discipline must also be proportional to the crime, and the offense must be explained. Unjust penalties stoke unnecessary resentment.

Children using drugs and alcohol are every parent's secret nightmare. It starts at school. It was always on our mind when our children were in school. When our son was in high school, I happened to comment on a kid who happened to be very popular in his class. I asked why our son did not socialize with him or his group of friends. He quietly remarked, "If you only knew. Appearances are deceptive. These kids are not what they appear to be." Taken by surprise, I asked why appearances were deceptive. After some forceful prodding, he explained that the kid drank alcohol, did drugs, and sometimes sold them in school. We were quite clear about not tolerating alcohol or drugs and kept a close eye for any behavioral changes that would hint at any usage.

After our children left for college, we hoped for the best. Our son called from college the day before his twenty-first birthday to warn us about an upcoming event. Because he had reached drinking age, his friends were taking him to a local bar to take part in the ritual of "getting wasted." He assured us that one of the friends was the designated driver and that he would call us the next morning. The assurance did not lessen our worry, but we were proud of him for thinking of us. Today, neither of our children is more than an occasional drinker.

I have never tasted alcohol other than being given brandy as a child for severe colds. It has not been a religious choice but something that my guru-ji (spiritual guide) advised against. He was not in favor of any stimulants in the form of alcohol or recreational drugs.

Another concern for me was what it could do to my professional life if alcohol took over my life. Surgery is a very exacting profession, with a lot of ups and downs. There were many days I came home and longed to try alcohol to see what it would feel like. I was curious as to whether it would lift my spirits like it seemed to do for people around me. I resisted, and the older I got, the less I desired it. How could I be sure that I could control myself if I began using drugs and alcohol? That has been my line of reasoning with our children. So far they have managed to restrict themselves to social drinking.

We know parents who give their children their first drink with the rationale that if the alcohol is consumed at home the parents can keep an eye on the children. More power to you if you are that confident in the vagaries of youth. For some immigrants, alcohol is prohibited by religion, and for others social consumption is acceptable. Whatever your preference, you can be sure that your children will be invited, coerced, and tempted. They will be curious about alcohol. It is important that you talk to them about the reasons for not drinking, if that is what you are going to advise them.

Life lessons: Set high expectations. Hypocrisy will destroy all the rules you have created and have asked your children to abide by. You are going to be disappointed occasionally, but concentrate on the issues that really matter. Separate the punishment for misbehavior from surrounding children with love.

TRUE VALUE: IT'S JUST A PIECE OF METAL!

The value attached to our children must be demonstrably apparent to them. In a materialistic world with expensive things all around us, it is easy to place an emphasis on objects. Often, objects are over-valued, while by implication, children are unintentionally under-valued. We have always de-emphasized the value of material things.

It was hard to impart that message to my children when we were living in a large house and possessed most conveniences of life, such as cars, televisions, and gadgets. Yet, it is possible to separate yourself from possessions and how much value you attach to them.

Our daughter had an auto accident shortly after she started to drive. Her car was hit by another car at a traffic light when the other car tried to turn against oncoming traffic. Our daughter's main concern when I arrived at the scene after receiving her call was how upset we were going to be with her for the damage to her new car. The first thing I said was to ask, "Are you all right?" Her response was to point out the damage to the car. My answer was, "It's just a piece of metal." That response and subsequent similar statements sunk into the mush of our children's brains. I have noticed this comment or something similar being uttered by our children when they damage some possession. When they lose or break an electronic gadget, they do not react with an exaggerated sense of loss, as is common in their generation.

The whole idea is to put the value of loved ones in perspective and material things in their proper place.

Life lessons: Show how much you value your children. Most parents do, but too few make obvious the priceless nature of their children. Compared to trivial objects, the physical and mental wellbeing of your children is incalculable. They need to know that.

DEALING WITH DISCRIMINATION, RACISM, AND BIGOTRY

Our son came home one day when he was about fifteen years old with a question. "What is a 'sand nigger'?" It seems he had gone with a friend to his school and met up with some kids on the street. A kid that often hung out with him had referred to him by that epithet. Our son was puzzled because he did not understand how someone who was pleasant enough while in his company could call him a name that sounded so racist. The second part of the epithet he understood, but the "sand" part took some explaining. I told him that it had to do with people who rode camels and lived in deserts where there was a lot of sand around. It hurt him that this person appeared to be friends with him and an African-American friend on the surface. It took some explanation out of my personal experiences.

There is ample evidence that acceptance of new immigrants by the host country is slower if there is a significant difference in body characteristics between the two.[6] Akhtar points out that immigrant children are particularly vulnerable to discrimination based on physical characteristics.

In my case it was skin color and ethnicity. I grew up as a religious minority. My entire childhood, into college, was spent trying to avoid my name being called in class. The name was a clear give away that I was not part of the majority religion. Initially it made me ashamed of my name. Later as I grew up, this shame was replaced by a resolve to be better than my tormentors were and show them what I was made of. There were jokes about kafirs (non-believers in Islam), idol worship, going straight to hell, and frequent invitations to convert to Islam. Fortunately, I had a couple of moderate Muslim friends who supported me, and their friendship has continued for over forty years.

Bigotry has existed in some form in the Indian Sub-continent and most other developing countries for centuries. The upper caste denigrated the lower caste. Direct descendants of religious prophets were set against the mere mortals. Fairer skinned people were prejudiced against the darker people. The keepers of the faiths (priests) looked down on the not-so-clean followers. There is bigotry and discrimination all across the world.

I was aware of these issues in my native country, but I did not expect to encounter it so openly in the United States. My first surprise was the barely visible "Blacks Only" sign at a water fountain in the emergency room at the large county hospital I rotated at in my first year in surgery. It certainly clashed with the pre-conceived impression I had from American movies, comics, and books about an open society. I was even more surprised to see discrimination alive and well in a top notch medical training institution. Being from a third world country meant a lot of people thought I was poor and was here for money. I had to explain that my family was very comfortable, with a large house, cars, and servants.

In my fourth year of training, I was passed over for a prime surgical rotation at the prestigious university hospital because I might not "fit in." My disgruntlement reached the chairman, who called me on the carpet and warned me to keep quiet or else I would not find a job anywhere in the U.S. He was a famous and powerful figure in American surgery. Some years later, he proudly gave me his picture with words to the effect that I had done a magnificent job.

When I applied after my residency program for a post-graduate fellowship at the same institution, a white Southern gentleman from outside the system was selected when the norm was to select an applicant from within the healthcare system. I was subsequently rejected at another Southern institution for advanced training for nebulous reasons. That only increased my resolve to work twice as hard and prove my detractors wrong. I stayed on at the university for another year in a different specialty than I wanted because I could not find a postgraduate position in the specialty of my choice. My director allowed me to spend two months out of my year working side by side with the southern, white candidate they had chosen. At the end of the rotation, the contrast between us was so obvious that the director who had made the decision to reject me allowed that he had made a mistake.

Many years later I was offered a faculty job at the same institution. I took pleasure in turning down the offer. Persistence and the determination to demonstrate my competence did change minds and hearts. The same chairman who threatened me for speaking out did me a huge favor, unbeknown to me. When I eventually did get a fellowship position in the Midwest in 1977, I wondered how the fellowship director had overlooked my ethnic background. He later told me that the only reason he gave me the job was because my chairman, who was a star in American Surgery, had called him and offered to pay my salary for the entire year if I failed at my job. The director had never heard of an offer like this. I did manage to change some minds.

I suppose I should not have been surprised that bigotry existed, even among highly educated physicians. During my private practice in the 1980s, there were two or three surgeons who always cracked inappropriate racist jokes in the lounge, targeting the minority that was not present at the time. Most of us learned to show our displeasure by simply walking away while the joke was in progress.

Most times, how someone acted was more indicative about how they felt towards me. I had been promised a partnership by my program director and boss during my last year of training or fellowship. I had also been called upon to perform surgery on him as well as on his daughter in an emergency while he was out of town. Most trainees complete their training at the end of June each year and therefore start hunting for jobs in early spring. Since I was assured of the job, I waited for a contract.

After July passed, knowing that almost all new jobs had been filled, my boss called to speak to me. He said he had changed his mind. He offered to pay me a large salary but declined to make me an equal partner at a later stage as was customary. The implication to me was that I was good enough to operate on him and his daughter and to be paid generously but not good enough to be his equal. I assumed that came from his impression that, being from a third world country, I had probably not seen this kind of money. He thought that I knew that, as a foreigner with my background, I would be unable to secure a good job at that late hour. I indicated to him that I was not lusting after money and did not want to work *for* him but *with* him as equal. Fortunately, another hospital wanted me to start my practice right away.

The "uppity" behavior did not sit well with my boss. He tried to blackball me from joining a prestigious national professional organization by calling in some chips. Enough surgeons of national stature stood behind my application, and his attempts to stop my application did not succeed. We occasionally run into each other and exchange pleasantries.

Some immigrants encounter similar behavior, with the presumption that they are here because they are poor and have never seen such wealth. Therefore, they should be grateful to be given money instead of equality in governance. Children of immigrants, if they look different from the majority, will encounter similar behavior. The parent needs to be ready to explain, support, and inject confidence back into them.

Our daughter went to a private school for girls after our initial attempt to get her a good education at our public school failed. The private school was predominantly white, and she had a difficult time sorting out her position among all the children from rich families. Almost all of her friends were white. The education was excellent, and we convinced her to complete her schooling. She has not gone back to any class reunion and has very few friends from the school. Although I do not recall her relating any overt racist behavior, I do think it shaped her thinking towards issues dealing with race. Her current friends are a healthy mix of people of all colors and races.

We have had many discussions about dealing with adversity and the best responses to similar incidents based upon my personal experiences. Anger and the impulse to immediately retaliate are natural. However, more can be accomplished by a calculating and thoughtful response.

The challenge to react with restraint has continued. Recently, my wife and I were asked to move from the exit row seats on a flight from John F. Kennedy International Airport by a white stewardess. First she said that "You look tired," and then "The passengers may not be able to understand your English in an emergency."

I had trouble understanding where she was going with this conversation at first. When I comprehended her unsaid concern, I asked, "Why don't you say what's on your mind? I can speak better English that you can." I did not tell her I was a professor of surgery at a major university. It was obvious that it was all about a foreign appearance rather than the English language. She finally walked away exclaiming, "Whatever."

I decided that we would exchange seats with a couple behind us dressed in Santa outfits. Across the aisle, in the other emergency seats, were two teenagers who had heard the conversation. One of them gave me her name and phone number to use in a complaint. We finally did get an apology from the airline after they received an angry letter from our senator. A similar complaint to the Department of Transportation resulted in their acceptance of the airlines explanation that we looked too tired to sit in the exit row seats. However angry the incident made me, I explained to our children that this did not make everyone a racist, and I was not about to condemn all security measures of the Department of Homeland Security. My country is more important than my feelings. I made it a point when relating my experience to my children to emphasize that I did not act like a victim, nor did I wallow in self-pity.

Along the same lines, I do not believe in a quota system and would be insulted if I was picked because of my color or ethnic origin. I do get angry at ignorance, but I have been vindicated later in every instance.

I suppose growing up as a minority has given me greater appreciation for the first, fourth, and fifteenth amendments to the U.S. Constitution. Perceptions differ, depending on which side of the ethnic/racial divide you happen to be on. Minorities, in general, tend to believe that they must be more qualified than are others to move up the career ladder. In a survey of healthcare executives, almost all whites disagreed with the idea that minority executives had to be more qualified to get promoted. In contrast, 66 percent of black, 35 percent of Hispanic and 33 percent of Asian men felt that they needed to be better qualified than whites to move up the ladder.[7]

Stereotyping is common in all cultures. We assume an over generalization about a particular group to be true for the entire group, without accounting for individual differences. For example, Asians are considered to be nerds, studious, always choosing technical careers, and generally affluent. Like other groups, immigrants are also stereotyped, depending on which part of the world they come from.

However, I have always emphasized to our children that most people are fair and will overlook ethnicity and race. In almost thirty years of medical practice, I have been aware of only a few instances where patients cancelled their appointments or expressed a desire to see a person of another color. I am sure there have been other instances that I did not know about, but, on the whole, the majority of my patients were white, and I am convinced that race and ethnicity became irrelevant to them after our first meeting.

Further, despite some negative personal experiences in the United States, I am reassured that there are legal remedies for direct and indirect discrimination, as well as for harassment and victimization. In most countries, there are no real remedies, so you have to either tolerate the injustice or move away, if that option is available. I know of people in some countries who have simply disappeared at night from their homes. Your children have to learn to deal with discrimination as a motivator and not take the easy route by feeling like a victim.

Life lessons: People can be hurtful because they are ignorant. You cannot stop them from being racist, but you can control the way you react. Prove to them you are better than they are. Success is the best form of revenge. Playing the victim does nothing to defeat ignorance and bigotry. I am not sure we can completely eliminate racism and bigotry in our lifetime, but hearts do change over time, even if some people will never be able to look beyond skin color.

HOLDING GRUDGES

He alone sees truly who sees the Lord the same in every creature, who sees the deathless in the hearts of all that die. Seeing the same Lord everywhere, he does no harm to himself or others. (*Bhagavad-Gita* 13:27-28)

I certainly had feelings of anger and promised myself that I would exact revenge against people who had treated me differently because of my ethnicity. We all know people we do not like. We do not hate them, but we simply do not like them. When things get testy with people like that, we tend to hold on to grudges when we are wronged. I also have a problem with getting angry when I feel I have been wronged. Then, I promise to hold a grudge and repay that person later. The problem is that when the time comes, I cannot bring myself to retaliate, so I decide to simply let it go. My daughter claims it's because I have class.

Certainly, we have a right to be angry at someone who violates our trust or tries to harm us or our reputation. The initial response tends to be from the gut, but that response, as most people learn, is often an over-reaction.

I have often said that, in this day of computers and e-mail, we should be prohibited from hitting the *reply* button in our email folder for twenty-four hours. That does two things. First, if the issue is that important, why not call the person? E-mail is so impersonal, and since we are not facing the other person or talking person to person on the phone, it is easy to say things you would never say otherwise. Second, the extra time is necessary for you to cool down, rethink the issue, and deliver a more measured response. I have been embarrassed several times, and often I wish I had a parental block on my computer. It does make one feel better to have delivered a response. However, mostly it does nothing to resolve the original problem.

Life lessons: Relate your experiences to your children by all means, but counsel patience and thoughtfulness. The impulse to retaliate against someone who has wronged you is your right. However, most times it may not be worth your time or energy. Things have a way of working out if you have patience and faith in your abilities.

MAINTAIN A LOW PROFILE

One's ego is like a shadow. It is always with us, sometimes larger than us, sometimes hiding and invisible, but always there. In Sufism, the ego is regarded as the last barrier before being one with God. Humility is very hard for most of us. Despite being aware of my guru-ji's teachings, I have often succumbed to public displays of wealth or tooting my own horn. I even had a vanity car license plate and owned a Mercedes Benz because I had always wanted to drive one. I attempt to fight my ego whenever an opportunity is thrown at me, but I do not always succeed.

Every now and then I get irritated when someone tries to impress me about a particular accomplishment. Worse is the person who retells me for the tenth time about how his child is at Harvard or working at a top notch international consulting firm. One acquaintance always manages to bore me with a pedestrian scientific study or paper he has had published. After several episodes, I finally had to put an end to the recitation by telling him that I had books in print and more than a hundred scientific publications. Although I liked seeing the reaction on his face, which told me he had no idea I was capable of these accomplishments, I immediately rebuked myself for letting my ego get the best of me.

I wonder what the purpose is when friends repeatedly hit you over the head with the fact that their children are attending Harvard or Princeton. Are they trying to prove that their genetic code is superior, or that they are better parents? Neither of our children went to an Ivy League school, but I would put them against a Harvard graduate, especially in the *better human being* category. Unfortunately, that category does not exist in any popular culture rating system.

We have tried to teach our children to keep a low profile, as far as displaying wealth or braying about their talents. I see a lot of physicians and other professionals repeatedly mentioning the value of their homes, cars, watches, and other possessions. No one likes someone who boasts about how much he or she is worth, especially if the listener is not financially at par with the blowhard. Such bragging may be expected of Hollywood elitists, but when it comes out of the mouths of someone else, it just makes the person seem more worthy of pity than envy. I think children notice how you deal with success as much as they watch you react to failures in life.

Life lessons: It is hard to keep your ego under control when you are flying high and want the world to know how successful you are. At least try to make an effort to keep it under control. Children need to learn to minimize public displays of wealth. Celebration of success in life is perfectly acceptable. It is the rubbing of success in other people's faces that is not necessary. Dealing with adversity in a hopeful and resolute manner is even more important as a lesson to be taught to children.

LEARNING FROM FAILURE

In my native culture, failure is not generally considered to be a learning opportunity. This seems to be a uniquely American value. Immigrants in the

U.S. soon learn that people may have failed in business or academics; yet, fewer stigmas are attached to failure than in other countries. Immigrant parents need to extol the virtues of the enormous opportunities in this country and free the children from the baggage of a fear of failure. People in North America are not afraid to take chances. Instead, they use failures as opportunities to learn and find a way to succeed.

One of the best ways for immigrants to teach their children about growing and succeeding in life is to enroll them in sports. It is a certainty that they will fail sometimes in competing at a sport. However, they will see other children continue to try hard after striking out in baseball or not making the class team. If the parent reinforces the message that the effort is worth it, the child will eventually succeed, and one taste of success at any level will be like a high they will remember. Playing sports also makes them interact with other children, who then tend to forget about the fact that they look different.

Life Lessons: Tear you self away from the thought patterns with which your parents and relatives viewed failure. Even if you freak out in private (as you will) be careful to be entirely supportive of good faith efforts by your children. I do not mean you should enable them to accept sloth, but if the effort is evident, you should encourage them by supporting them while they try again and again.

IS THE GLASS HALF EMPTY OR HALF FULL?

Being thankful to our Creator is another very basic tenet of my faith, regardless of the ups and downs of life. Practicing this advice under adverse circumstances is a lot harder than hearing someone preach it. Children are well aware of differences between the media images of wealth, possessions, titles, and name recognition and the relative importance parents assign to these things in the family's value system. You never want to share envy you may have about another person. Instead, talk about what you have been blessed with, or what the other person has. That teaches children about your values system.

For example, it has never bothered me that people I know are a lot richer or better known than I am. What I tell myself when envious thoughts do seep into my consciousness is that others do not have what is dear to me: my ideal marriage; two of the best children I could ask for; my guru-ji, who I believe is my salvation; and everything I could possibly want.

Children need to hear this or, better, deduce these values from your behavior or response when others are envious of fame and fortune. They need to learn to ask themselves whether they would want a share in the other person's fame or fortune if it meant taking on their problems. If children comment on what a beautiful and large house someone has, my response would be to remind them of what the taxes and maintenance on that house is must be. If they are envious of some Hollywood celebrity's fame, I would comment on the unhealthy culture in Hollywood and its hypocrisy, saying, "No thanks."

Life lessons: Children need to understand that they are given their share of blessings and that wishing for someone else's share shows ingratitude and just make's one miserable. They need to look at their strengths and be thankful.

VALUE OF MONEY

The need of affluent parents to teach children about the value of money is even greater now. These days a teenager without a cell phone, an IPOD, a laptop, and even a television with cable in their own room often considers herself to be living without the basic necessities of life. We were blessed to have enough to live in a decent house, to have cars, and to be able to afford private school and a few vacations with our children. The problem was frequently how to deal with demands for the latest gadgets, brand name shoes, and CDs their friends possessed. When we suggested that something was not necessary, we were told, "All our friends have it" or "You can afford it," based upon our affluence.

We did what was necessary to satisfy their needs within limits. However, frequently, they distinctly understood that we could afford to buy what they wanted but chose not to. Like most parents, we opened savings accounts for them, and they deposited their wages and gift money from relatives into the account. In our culture, children are given money by older relatives when they visit them in the Indian sub-continent. Grandparents, uncles, and aunts all shove money into their grubby little hands, which is then counted, converted into dollars and then deposited into their bank accounts in the United States.

Our children had enough money that they did not feel deprived, but we made sure they did not have money to waste. We rarely paid for designer goods. They often paid for the extras or contributed towards things they wanted that were more expensive than I was willing to spend. We almost never surrendered our credit card to them. There were very few exceptions when cash simply would not have been safe. As they grew up, I became more generous and told them that I would rather give them money for their needs while I was alive then leave them too much after I was gone. Still, the generosity was not over-done but covered their replacement cars, down payment for their condos/houses, shortfalls every now and then, overseas trips, and occasional vacations. I disputed uncalled-for finance charges, as little as a dollar with banks and credit card companies. I wanted to show them that I was fighting for my hard-earned money.

I think it is clear that they need to understand the value of money.

Most parents teach children about money by using money as a motivator. If the incentive is seen as fair, such as a reward for washing a few dishes or sweeping the garage, it is reasonable to use money as a motivator. It becomes a problem when it is seen as unfair. What seems unfair can vary from individual to individual.[8] Another issue, often observed in the work environment, is that sometimes money becomes an expected entitlement. If your children expect money out of proportion to the chore, it is not a motivator.

Teaching children about money starts early in life. In lower school grades, they should be taught the value of an allowance in exchange for simple chores. Verbalize how you make financial decisions in very easy to understand terms. This may also be the time to talk about helping those less fortunate than your family. Encourage your children to become a part of any charitable activity that you and your spouse support. It may be a stint at the local food bank or a soup line. One parent described how he would encourage children to find the cheapest gallon of gas, while driving them to school. Later, his teenage daughter asked him for the grocery store card that gave a ten cent discount on each gallon of gas.

In middle school, teach them about responsibility by opening a savings account at your bank. They will get familiar with the process of banking, watch their savings grow, learn about interest and also about taxation on any earnings. You will be raising their allowance. Children, at this stage are starting to ask for things you may not be willing to pay for. They will learn about making smart choices in buying things with limited resources. They may want extra chores at home or in the neighborhood to be able to earn more to afford their object of desire.

When children enter high school the demand for expensive trinkets goes up. At this stage, they are able to hold a part-time job in the summer and learn to drive. It is a perfect time to teach them about establishing a proper credit history.

A pre-paid credit card or a debit card is probably the safest vehicle for them. Credit card law requires that those under twenty-one years of age have parents take responsibility for a card unless the child has enough income to qualify personally. This involves some risk. If this bothers you, you can make them an authorized user on one of your credit cards.

Another option is the use of a secured credit card. This requires that the child (or parent) makes a deposit, which becomes the card's limit. This type of card does carry an annual fee and occasionally a setup charge. Generally there is no grace period, which means the card company will charge interest on purchases immediately. Children will need to learn about exorbitant interest rates, late fees and how credit scores are derived. In a recent survey of 200 freshmen, 58 percent possessed a credit card but more than 60 percent only used it sparingly for necessary items and paid balances in full. The study also reports that 70 percent reported "financially risky" behavior. The researchers point out that parental interaction has a great influence on subsequent student behavior.[9]

The problem is that using the credit card sparingly is wonderful, but students still need to demonstrate a good credit history. Lack of a responsible credit history makes it difficult for lenders to approve loans for apartments, cars, and insurance policies.

As your children think of the money as theirs, they should become stingier with it.

By the time they head for college, you should have taught them to be responsible for their own expenses, and they have learned to exercise some discipline with their finances. They will still need financial assistance, but, in exchange, you have to ask for transparency and accountability in how they spend the money. I do not mean asking for a spreadsheet with every nickel listed. Instead, they should give an informal run down by having them list their monthly expenses in broad categories of housing, books, food, entertainment, and travel. This exercise helps them think about how they are spending the money, and any significant outlays will make them conscious of overspending without you even pointing it out.

In all this, make sure you and your spouse are joined at the hip about saying no to repeated demands for more money that will come your way.

I believe this approach has also made our children better consumers. They both learned to clip coupons, ask lots of questions before buying articles, reject most warranties, bargain for low prices, and write complaint letters to companies over defective products. Their favorite story about me concerns my complaint to a well know cereal maker. I once opened a box of cereal and found what looked like a dead insect. I enclosed the dead insect in a letter to the cereal maker and got a quick response. My daughter learned well. When her Honda Civic turned out to be a lemon, she collected a bunch of bills related to her engine and complained loudly enough that Honda reimbursed her over $1500, even though the car was way past the warranty period. That's my daughter.

Life lessons: If you have lots of money it is easy to slip into excessive generosity so they will like you and so you can avoid arguments. If you do not, you will still be under pressure to get them just one more thing that their friends have! Be consistent. Put up a common front and do not let them play you against each other. Teach them to be good consumers.

FRUGALITY AND DEBT

I have never been in debt (other than the mortgage on the house) and always paid all bills on time. Credit cards are to be used for convenience and not for buying things when I did not have money in the bank to pay for them. Americans are burdened with over $6.5 trillion in consumer debt. Personal debt as a ratio of Gross Domestic Product has gone from 60 percent in 1990 to 100 percent.[10] Our personal debt is now equal to our national Gross Domestic Product. Worse, young adults do not understand the difference between *nominal* (annual percentage) interest rates of 18 percent versus *periodic* rates that may be calculated monthly not annually, often pushing rates to 30 percent to 40 percent.

These days, immigrants from even poor countries are familiar with credit cards, though they may not have owned or used them. If you are used to dealing in cash, debt is a stressful necessity of life in the United States. Unfortunately, our children see that all their friends use their credit cards as a loan machine and, as a result, pay exorbitant interest rates. You have to teach them to ignore an average of seven solicitations they get in the mail for credit cards every year, not counting numerous web pages with flashing "click here" ads for easy credit. Our children have moved away from the advice we received that housing expenses should not consume more than 25 percent of monthly income. You see them shopping at electronics stores carting away those sixty-inch plasma televisions.

It starts with teaching them to save. This should go beyond money to a general attitude about saving everything, including food, water, and energy. How do you hammer frugality into children when all their friends are living in the land of instant gratification? My children saw me sew buttons on myself and patch parts of shoes so I could continue to wear them. They knew I could afford to buy new clothes and shoes. They saw me ask my wife to mend a few shirts. I took possession of my son's t-shirts, which were in reasonably good condition, when he decided they were out of fashion. Our daughter wore socks with holes in them for a long time, until we laughed and said she could afford new pairs of socks.

Take your children to the store to teach them to be better shoppers. Clipping coupons when they know you can afford not to, sends a powerful message. Turning lights off when leaving a room or re-using supplies is consistent with your message. Eating out three days a week and paying top dollar confuses them when you are trying to get them to save their allowance. When shopping for a big ticket item like a computer or television, get them involved in checking out prices and value by comparison shopping on Web sites and in magazines. I am not sure my wife and I succeeded in teaching our children frugality to the extent I would have liked, but we certainly tried.

Life lessons: Reinforce your message of frugality at every turn. There is a difference between not denying yourself necessities of life when you can afford to have them and splurging beyond your means. The concept of saving money for a rainy day is critical, and must be taught at an early age. Your job is to reiterate the message as often as you can. This lesson will be repeatedly wiped clean by slick advertising, the temptation to keep up with friends when they spend beyond their means, and falling prey to a media message to live right now, without concern for the future.

INDIVIDUAL RESPONSIBILITY

Most immigrants do not come expecting handouts. They fully expect to work and take responsibility for themselves and their families. Where most of them come from, governments do not provide much help for the average person. The concepts of welfare, state-run assistance programs, food stamps, public housing, and free health care are all new to them. Imagine their wonder when their friends and relatives inform them that all these programs are available to them. Some take the easy route and get used to the easy life, while others have so much pride in their ability to provide for their families that they look with disdain at their friends who receive such help.

I was taught to take responsibility for myself at an early age. There was no one else to blame. Blaming God or the government was not an option. I have tried to instill the same values in our children. While I have sympathy with those unable to provide for themselves, I accept fewer excuses than most people I know, except for those with genuine disabilities. If you take such a stance, your children may think you are closer in your thinking to Attila the Hun when it comes to personal responsibility. However, children may see the term *personal responsibility* in a political context and meant to be used to assist the poor and disadvantaged.

My context is entirely different. I do not care whether those under discussion are the poor or the rich, the native or the immigrant, black or white. I can be as empathic as the next person, but I think I know when someone is offering a lame excuse and blaming something or someone else for personal irresponsibility. I just emphasize trying to take responsibility for yourself and your family. Like most parents, we asked and encouraged our children to work at an early age. They worked at the state fair, fast food restaurants, car electronic shops, prosecutor's offices, lawn mowing and leaf blowing.

There is nothing as satisfying to a parent as when they see their teenager watch his or her bank balance increase with a real pay check and decline due to taxes.

Life lessons: Most immigrants are proud people who come here for various reasons. One reason is usually that they want to better the lives of their children. Still, they want to raise their children with the same philosophy they were raised with—the importance of taking personal responsibility. Certainly, temporary assistance should be availed upon when faced with disability or serious illness, but work in any form to provide for one's family is an obligation.

EMPATHY

I was struck with differences in dealing with patients from the first month I was in the U.S. Being from an under-developed country, I was totally unprepared for the technology and gadgetry, the new generation of drugs, and the medical terminology. I went around on patient rounds the first day with a group of interns and residents supervised by a chief resident (a fifth- or final-year trainee in surgery). We would stand at the foot of the patient beds, and the intern would read off the vital signs and laboratory and radiologic reports to the chief. The chief would then talk briefly to the patients (sometimes), make suggestions about treatment, and move to the next bed. There was almost no patient contact. Such treatments as antibiotics for pneumonia were ordered based on plain x-rays of the chest. Lacking the fancy diagnostic tool of x-rays in my native country, I was used to listening to the patient's chest after talking to him about his complaints and progress. I continued to practice what I had been taught, which was to talk to patients, getting to know them and their problems.

One night on call, I was called to the intensive care unit to do a "cut-down" on an arm vein of an elderly woman. No one could find a vein to start an intravenous line and the woman had already had a couple of cut-downs, where someone would have to cut and find a vein in her fore-arm. I followed my usual practice of entirely numbing the area with local anesthetic and started the intravenous line very quickly.

The patient was shocked when I told the nurse I was finished. She then explained that the other times this procedure had been done to her she suffered excruciating pain. This was the first time someone had given her enough local anesthetic.

She then said to me, "Honey, give me some sugar." I gave her a blank look, whereupon she said it again. I turned to the nurse with a questioning stare.

The nurse concluded that I was new and explained, "Mrs. S would like to have you give her a kiss on her cheek." We remained friends for many years after she left the hospital. She taught me many American expressions such as "ten four" and "a tad."

Life lessons: My experience in medicine has been that immigrant physicians, in general, exhibit a lot of empathy, although that is a broad generalization. Let us as parents pass this trait on to our children. You want your children to be great professionals, wonderful parents, and successful members of society, but you should be prouder if they turn out to be worthy of being called good human beings.

Many immigrants are used to closed spaces with many people around them. They are accustomed to having little privacy. They are taken aback at the private space that people in the U.S. maintain. The difference is reflected in relationships, neighborhoods, and work places.

There is a tendency that bad days are shared between friends and neighbors more commonly in other countries than I have observed in the U.S. Kind acts are undoubtedly taking place each day, but feelings are kept in check. Empathy for friends, relatives, and neighbors is simply more commonly expected by immigrants when relating to each other.

Even though it is not discouraged by any means, showing empathy and acting on those feelings is a little awkward for new immigrants when they are receiving mixed signals from others. Immigrant parents are therefore confused about what they should teach their children. They are not sure how this behavior will be received by their American friends and neighbors.

Life lessons: Children get used to doing what they see practiced at home. A good reason for them to visit their relatives or grandparents in their native countries is to observe this behavior and learn to share their private space.

PRIDE IN YOUR ETHNICITY AND SELF-ESTEEM

"Ethnicity refers to the culture of a people and includes values, child rearing practices, sense of history, modes of expression, and patterns of interpersonal behavior."[11] Pride in ethnicity and roots is a matter of actively conveying and exhibiting cultural traditions. Conveying ethnicity to your children includes exposing them to ethnic events, music, food, movies, books, and like-minded friends. This becomes harder when children reach adolescence, as they are pulled into the magnetic field of the way of life of school, friends, and exposure to the media.

The same influences that are attractive to adolescents also may work to lower their self-esteem. The children may see their own ethnicity and culture as inferior and actually participate with others who make fun of the food, smells, clothing, and religion associated with their parents. They do this so they can fit in with their friends and do not have to defend their own ethnicity.

Immigrant parents find it hard to deal with their children's newly found autonomy and rebellion at this stage and may over-react with threats to return to their native country, send the children (particularly females) back home, or, in the extreme, brandish physical punishment.

I was raised in a very traditional family, in which parents raised their children more by gut instinct than a well-thought-out plan. Children in our culture often live with their parents even after marriage as a joint family unit where parents play a prominent role in any decision. No conscious thought is given to building a child's self-esteem. All my wife and I knew when our children came along was that they should truly believe that they were loved, regardless of their actions, thoughts, or decisions. We felt they needed to be confident of our love in order to deal with the challenges that life was going to put in front of them. Also, our thinking was that if, our children were encouraged to like themselves, be confident in their abilities, and believe in themselves, that they would be resilient enough to handle adversity. We felt this was all the more important since they looked different from most of their peers.

They have certainly inherited from us introspection, internal criticism, and a tendency to over-do self-examination. However, we tried to emphasize their positive qualities to bolster their self-esteem. We think it has worked.

Life lessons: Pay attention to the change in children as they grow into adolescence. Keep them engaged and connected to their ethnicity. Sooner or later, pride in their own culture will begin to show. Remember that they are undergoing a more intense period of self-examination than you did. Their burden is heavier and different. By all means, criticize your child's behavior, but always direct criticism with a view to making it a teaching moment. If some action is wrong, then what is right? The message should be that they are better than the action you just criticized.

NOTES

1. "Values," from "WordNet, A Lexical Database for English" Princeton University, http://wordnetweb.princeton.edu/perl/webwn?s=values.

2. "What Are Values?" *University of Cincinnati Magazine* (August 2005), http://www.magazine.uc.edu/0805/whatarevalues.htm.

3. Thomas A. Atchison, *Leadership's Deeper Decisions* (Chicago: Health Administration Press, 2006).

4. "Mission Coach, Coaching on Purpose," Change in Mind Ltd., www.missioncoach.co.uk.

5. Atchison, *Leadership's Deeper Decisions*.

6. Salman Akhtar, *Immigration and Identity: Turmoil, Treatment and Transformation* (Lanham, MD: Jason Aronson, 1999), 27.

7. Peter Weil, "A Race/Ethnic Comparison of Career Attainments in Healthcare Management," *Healthcare Executive* (November/December 2003): 21-27.

8. Atchison, *Leaderships deeper decisions*.

9. "Financial Train Wrecks: Study Finds Parents May Be Young People's Top Defense," Arizona Pathways to Life Success for University Students (APLUS) study, http://tcainstitute.org/PR_APLUS_Published.pdf. Karen Blumenthal, "Teaching Kids about Money the Hard Way," *Wall Street Journal,* July 16, 2009, http://www.online.wsj.com/article/SB10001424052970203739404574286821533215800.html.

10. Steve Hamm, "The New Age of Frugality,"*Businessweek*, October 20, 2008, http://www.businessweek.com/magazine/content/08_42/b4104054847273.htm.

11. Salman Akhtar and C. Hughes C, "Culture in Clinical Psychiatry," in *Culture, Ethnicity and Mental Illness*, ed. A. C. Gaw (Washington, DC: American Psychiatric Press, 1993), 3-42

Chapter Four

Education, Education, and Education

My father was one of the few people in our circle of family and friends to go beyond high school. His family managed large swaths of agricultural lands and did not have any college graduates in the family. He was the first and ahead of his time. He received a bachelor's degree in arts. He wanted his kids to have the best education, no matter what it cost him. He searched far and wide for the best school in the country. He found one that met his criteria, which was situated in the mountains five hundred miles away. My mother protested that at ten I was too young to be by myself. But father was going to have his way, first born or not. A few relatives of high school age (sixteen to eighteen years old) had been sent to boarding schools in our extended family. So, it was a big deal indeed.

He took me by train to St. Francis Grammar School, a catholic run school, one of the best boarding schools in India and Pakistan in 1958. The narrow gauge train ran all night through many tunnels in a series of mountainous ranges and countless stops before arriving at the railway station. The city was picturesque, and the school was nestled in between mountains. The city had been the site of one of the most devastating earthquakes in recent history in 1935. There were memorials to the dead at the railway station and in the city.

The dormitory was one large room with about fifty cots. Strict rules were enforced about getting up, when lights would go out, taking showers so many times a week and finishing all the food on your plate. The most disgusting routine was scooping up beef dinners served on our plates into a news paper in my lap, hiding it and throwing it outside. The priest making the rounds in the dining room enforcing the rules did not care that Hindus were prohibited from eating beef. I remember being miserable the first few months, being lonely, and writing notes to my family demanding to be brought back home.

Or I asked for parcels and goodies to be sent. All kids waited for letters and parcels from home and compared goodies.

A few times a week a Pathan (an ethnic native of the mountainous area) would come by on a bicycle, selling pastries and rolls filled with cream. Most of my pocket money went toward stuffing me with these delicious goodies.

Two years later I was sent to a paramilitary school closer to home, run by a Britisher by the name of Colonel Coombs. Colonel Coombs was a large, jovial man who was a left over from the British Raj. The discipline here was much stricter, with reveille in the form of a bugle waking us up at six every morning. All students were expected to fend for themselves. There were surprise inspections to make sure shoes were polished, brass belt buckles were shining, and closet shelves were neat and dust free.

I was one of the youngest children there and the shortest. The teachers insisted on everyone participating in every sport, including boxing. I was put in the ring with a boy who was taller by at least four inches. The only way I survived was by being quick on my feet and running to the four corners before he could let loose any big punches. These experiences in self reliance were to come in handy when I arrived in Atlanta, Georgia, in 1972 without a soul to rely on.

Most families in the U.S. do not send their children to boarding schools. The first experience children have of living on their own is at mini-camps while they are in school or when they are packed off to college. Like other families, we also sent our children to tennis or soccer camps, but these camps were usually a few days long. Apprehension about being away from your children even for a few days is normal, but this is a great opportunity for them to mix and make friends outside their circle of siblings and cousins. Summer camps may give the children a chance to meet other children of similar cultures, who come from other schools and neighborhoods.

ENGLISH, ENGLISH, AND MORE ENGLISH

The school population has changed dramatically over the last two decades. As Laurie Olsen points out in *Made in America* that in California alone the school enrollment has shifted from 75 percent white to just under 40 percent white, with 25 percent of students limited in their ability to speak English.[1] Although there is no official language in the U.S., and the constitution does not mention anything in this regard, by default English has always been the preferred language. Those students who are not fluent in English are called 'limited English proficient' or LEP.

Olsen observes that the teacher profile has not changed to match the student population. There is a lot of variability in the background education of immigrant students. The differences often trace back to whether the student was educated in a poor rural area or in a middle-class or upper-middle-class urban area. The actual curriculum, the teaching style, and sequence of subjects are vastly different. Commonly students from a less-adequate school background feel that, no matter how hard they try, they are not "American" due to their culture, religion, accent, clothing or skin color. The English language, clothes, and music are seen as the most powerful symbols of being "American."

Learning and mastering the English language is the most important tool for immigrant students. Parents who are themselves deficient have to dedicate themselves to improving their own skills. They are torn between speaking English or their native language at home. If they insist on speaking their native language they risk marginalizing their children when they go to school.

However, they feel guilty of abandoning their heritage as their formerly LEP children gradually shift from thinking in their native language to speaking, thinking and dreaming in English.

At this stage, parents may focus on the prejudice they may encounter. Any discussion about race, color, and religion makes most immigrant students uncomfortable. First, they may not feel comfortable responding with the truth. Second, the conversation has to be eased into gently. Perhaps it is framed around a discussion about a television program, a book, or a news story in the newspaper. Children are trying desperately to merge in with the majority, and it is important that, although the discussion is serious and needs to occur, the conversation needs to flow casually.

Life lessons: Your first priority is to make sure your children master the English language. Do whatever it takes to ensure that they are totally comfortable with written and spoken English. Then, you can start conversing in your native language and trying to pass it on to them.

TEACHING STYLE

The grading system in the U.S. is very different from that in most countries outside the West. Most immigrant parents and children are familiar with either a pass or fail grade or, more likely, a numerical number assigned to a test, quiz, or examination. For example, a student might be given 80 "marks" out of a maximum of 100, which in the U.S. would probably equate to a *B* or a 3.0 Grade Point Average (GPA). A 90 score out of 100 is often termed a "first class" or "distinction" or "honors" in other countries. That would be equivalent to an *A* here (Table 4).

Table 4.   Equivalent School Grading Systems

U.S	Asian countries
A or a GPA of 4.0	First Class or Honors, generally 75% or above, some countries 90%
B or GPA 3.0	First Class, generally 60% score or above, some countries 80–90% score
C or GPA 2.0	Second Class, 45% or above score, some countries 75–79% score
D or GPA 1.0	Third Class, 30% score
F (fail)	Fail below 30% score, some countries below 75% score

Adapted from Leticia Gallares-Japzon, *Succeeding in America* (Silver Springs, MD: TeamCom Books, 2001).

The teaching style is very different from that of most other non-Western countries. Like other non-Western countries, my schooling was in a formal atmosphere where the teacher was god. Everyone was quiet and sat up straight, with no food or drinks allowed in the classroom. Attendance was taken by the teacher in the form of a roll call. The only way to get out of class was either by a medical note or by jumping out an adjacent window after roll call when the teacher's back was turned. Otherwise, you got into trouble at school. In the U.S. children interact with other children and teachers. Certainly in college they are often allowed to bring food or drinks inside the class room and to dress informally.

Children in the U.S. are encouraged to ask questions and speak up, whereas in other countries respect for teacher's leads to a formal environment where any attempt to converse informally is seen as disrespectful.

Teachers in the U.S. often tend to label immigrant children, even those who are fluent in English, as quiet, reserved, or even disinterested because they do not ask questions or engage in a free for all discussion in class. As the child's grades suffer, parents remain puzzled about their bright child's abilities. Parents sometimes need to take the initiative and ask to meet their child's teachers, just to take a pulse on how the child is engaging others at school.

Life lessons: Do not expect your children to learn in the same environment you did. That does not mean you don't insist on total respect for teachers, but you need to encourage them to speak up in class.

PRESSURES ON YOUR CHILDREN

The emphasis on education is pervasive in immigrant families. For instance, based on the U.S. census figures, 43 percent of Asian Americans as a group had college degrees, compared to 9.9-25.3 percent in other groups.[2] This partly accounts for the highest median income for their families of $59,000 annually, compared to $32,240-$48,500 a year for other groups.

Although the comparison may be somewhat misleading because these families may have a larger number of individuals working and bringing in income to the joint family, the affluence of Asian families is commonly mentioned in the media. What is forgotten is that there are also very poor families who live in miserable circumstances.

The image of Asians as a highly educated ethnic minority is advanced by such things as the number of Asians who are Rhodes Scholars. From 2000-2006, Asians have accounted for 23 of 132 (17.4 percent) of Rhodes scholars.[3] This is a higher number in relationship to the 4.2 percent of Asians in the general population.

However, the belief that, since Asians score higher on examinations such as the SAT compared to other ethnic groups they must be smarter, is a myth. Nisbett, in his book *Intelligence and How to Get It: Why Schools and Cultures Count*, explains that Asian accomplishments are more due to sweat and cultural differences. Obligation to one's family, for example, makes students work harder to bring honor to their families. In fact, there is almost too much pressure on children growing up as part of a model minority. There are also differences in the way Asians learn that parents need to be aware of as well. According to Nesbitt, East Asians for example, are dependent, holistic, and able to see things in context, compared to Westerners, who tend to be independent, analytic, and focus on the point at hand.

In essence he points out that Easterners are collectivistic in contrast to Westerners, who are individualistic.[4] This explains why the entire family owns and shares an honor (or dishonor) earned by their daughter or son.

The U.S. has allowed large numbers of Asians to immigrate based on their educational qualifications. The numbers decreased somewhat after passage of several pieces of legislation, such as the Immigration Act of 1990. In general though, the professional class of immigrants, as well as blue collar workers who came to the U.S. has emphasized education in their households.

Since my wife and I were both well educated, the expectation on our children was never far from the surface. We never screamed and hollered when they received suboptimal grades, but they knew when they had disappointed us. The pressure on them to get good grades was more than subtle. I do not think we ever directly compared them or their grades with our friend's children. That would have been counterproductive. Even after they were older and on their own, they remarked how intimidating it had been to try and meet the standard we had set for them. Neither one of us ever verbally suggested that they had to achieve similar goals. However, the non-verbal cues must have been obvious to them. A lot of the pressure was self-generated.

The issues are different when children go away to college. Besides the independent decisions they have to make, they now have to deal with money issues. As I have mentioned, you should have prepared them for this day. One issue for parents is that of paying for college. Parents start thinking about paying for college when the children are born. We did too. However, the discussion with children should start in high school. This gives them a clue about whether they should look at public or private colleges.

I believe that if parents can afford to pay for their children's college education, they should consider helping them. There is a balance between having them take responsibility for themselves versus making sure they concentrate on their studies, rather than worry about generating enough income to pay for food, lodging, and other necessities. We elected to establish an educational trust account, to which we contributed through their lower and middle school years. It helped pay for college and some graduate school expenses. For some parents, this may not be affordable, and loans for college are perfectly acceptable. This may elicit feelings of guilt in immigrants because they may feel they have let down their children.

We did encourage both children to take out some loans during graduate school. I think parents should discuss options for college funding with their children when they are finishing high school. If money has been saved for college, the discussion should be about whether to use the money to pay for college or graduate education. The advantage with an account is that, if investments within the account do well, there may be enough money to do both. But, if investments do poorly, they may have to earn enough money themselves to fund the remaining part of their education.

Life lessons: High expectations set by parents are perfectly acceptable as long as success or failure to achieve them is not perceived by children as being correlated with how much love they receive. I do not think it hurts children to have an internal desire to measure up to the high standards set by their parents. We all know of very successful people who have reached great heights without much education or sometimes even hard work. But, for the vast majority, success, however it is measured, does result from hard work, with or without education. Work habits are best instilled early. If a child decides to play football, be an artist, or try their luck on a fledgling technology venture, a good education serves as an insurance policy, just in case. This is an almost universal theme in immigrant families.

THE SCHOOL SYSTEM

Public education is free, universal, and compulsory throughout the United States at the primary and secondary level. The support for public schools comes from taxes. The state determines the age at which your child will be allowed to enter the first grade, although generally this ranges from six to seven years of age. Elementary school goes through the end of the fifth grade, middle school is through the end of the eighth grade and high school is from the ninth grade and ends after the twelfth grade.

The quality of the public education varies according to the school district in which you live. Another choice is private school, which you will have to pay for. The final choice is to home school your children, where you follow the state mandated curriculum and teach them at home.

COLLEGE OR UNIVERSITY

After graduation from high school (or twelfth grade), the choice is a public college or university versus a private institution, a community college, which normally requires two years to complete, or a vocational school. Which direction you take depends on many factors, including your finances, tuition assistance available, your child's grade point average (GPA), and special skills or talents your child possesses.

Vocational schools are for students who want to work with a particular trade, such as carpentry, mechanics, or an electrical field.

Helping your children choose a college or university for the first time is a daunting task for immigrant parents. The average American family also tends to be anxious about the process, but there is a good chance that the parents have gone through the process themselves. They understand the pros and cons of the factors that are important in choosing one college over another.

The stress for immigrants is multiplied because they have no idea what to look for and what questions to ask. They suffer from information overload at each college campus they visit. The family comes home with hundreds of pamphlets and brochures. At the end of the trip all the details are jumbled up. It is useful during these trips to jot down notes on what is specific to that campus. That will help you remember the pros and cons. It is a wonderful opportunity for parents to spend time with their child at one of the most important and exciting periods in their lives. We went as a family to visit colleges. We gathered as much information as possible ahead of time, planned a route on the map, and set out.

The trips were easier, as neither of our children wanted to go south or west, so we concentrated in the Midwest and the East Coast. Our daughter chose a small, very liberal college within an hour's driving distance from home. She gave up her car so she would avoid the temptation to come home too often.

Your children may assume that you will interfere with and micromanage their life at college if they have heard that immigrant parents do that. We surprised our daughter by not calling or visiting her very much, to the point that she asked whether we missed her. Most parents in our position would have made runs to her college with homemade food a couple of times a week. We decided to let her grow up on her own so that she would be ready to deal with life by herself. We wanted to serve as a backup. It worked.

Our son chose a large university over three hours away, which was huge compared to the small private secondary school he had attended. It took two semesters before he was comfortable and not home sick there. For parents, the younger child is usually much harder to separate from, and disconnecting may take longer.

CAREER CHOICE

"Find a job that you love and you will never work another day in your life." (Confucius)

Parents of children in most non-European countries have a big say in what careers their children choose. In addition, since most countries do not offer the range of choices the United States has, selection of a career in medicine or engineering for example, occurs very early, often in high school. So, most first-generation immigrants don't want to hear their children say, "I am not sure what I want to do" or even "I think I will become a designer."

My mind was made up at age fourteen. I suffered with renal colic throughout my late childhood years without a proper diagnosis. The bouts of severe flank pain left me rolling on the floor and caused me to miss many school days.

Eventually my father took me to Bombay, India, where a general surgeon by the name of Dr. Motwani diagnosed me as having a stone or benign growth that blocked the flow of urine from the kidney. The surgery was complicated and resulted in over a month in the hospital. The surgeon was an absolute angel. He was kind, empathic, and reassuring. I decide I wanted to be like him and help others. We later became friends, and he and his wife stayed with us when he visited the U.S.

My father always wanted me to be a physician. There had not been a physician in our family going back many generations. Our forefathers were land owners and managed agricultural properties, and no one had obtained a college degree until my father graduated with a Bachelor of Arts degree. I am not sure what direction I would have taken had my choice differed with my father's.

Many immigrants are well-educated professionals and are generally obsessed with the goal of having their children follow in their footsteps. A career choice outside established, secure professional careers, such as medicine, engineering, and business administration, strike most immigrant parents as being risky. They are likely to look down their noses at careers in fashion design, music, and art or even becoming a writer. Parents take special pride in telling friends in their communities about the Ivy League schooling they are paying for.

I am often asked why my kids did not opt for a career in medicine. The answer is that we left it up to them. Our children saw me work long hours, coming home exhausted and consumed by patient issues. Their mother pretty much had to handle most family problems on her own. That may have had some influence on their choice of careers. They are highly educated, but they chose other careers. It was a running joke in our family that we could only afford to have two people in the family in school at any one time. One person would graduate and be employed while another went back to school. My wife was in and out of school with two bachelor's degrees, one master's and an advanced degree in counseling. Our daughter has a bachelor's, a master's, and a PhD. Our son got his bachelor's, an MBA, and now that no one else is in school, he is trying to get into medical school.

Children growing up in the U.S. have such a wide range of choices that they are often confused about which road to take. It is common for children graduating from college to take a year or two off to decide what they want to for the rest of their lives. That seems like "slumming" to most immigrant parents. The parents fear what friends in the community are going to say. They see it as a defect in their child raising skills that resulted in their children being confused about their career choice. Lately, the stigma attached to taking time off after college is receding, as more children are using the time to be sure of their goals in life. If your child is also of this opinion, encourage him or her but stay involved to make sure the time is used wisely.

Life lessons: Other than total snobs, few Americans look down on professions that make a living doing manual labor or vocations other than medicine, engineering, or business. Children are, in fact, confused because the options are endless. Sometimes, it may take them several years to realize that the profession they chose was not what they had imagined. It is certainly aggravating for a parent who thought a child was now settled down to deal with a few more years of switching careers. The parent should try to understand their child's argument for making such a decision. Americans look at their education as a life-long process, believing that they would rather be happy with what they are doing rather than continue to suffer because of an earlier misjudgment.

SAVING FOR YOUR CHILDREN'S EDUCATION

Like most parents, immigrants want to plan for their children's educational needs. As I have mentioned, excellence in education is emphasized in many immigrant households. Parents are conscious of the cost of education beyond high school in the U.S. However, parents need to know that those with a bachelor's degree earn over 60 percent more than those with only a high school diploma. That translates to over $800,000 over a lifetime.[5]

At this writing, the cost of attending a public college is around $7,020 a year, up 6.5 percent from last year. For private colleges it is $26,273 a year (up 4.4 percent from last year).[6] Immigrant parents are not used to the number and varieties of scholarships available for needy students. There is also misinformation that a child is more likely to be eligible for a scholarship if his or her parents have not saved money.

Some basic information for parents is necessary to understand and deal with the U.S. educational assistance system.

First, let me explain terms.

Expected Family Contribution (EFC)

The EFC is information that helps financial aid counselors to determine the student's need for financial assistance. The EFC is the amount the student's family is capable of providing toward his or her college tuition and other expenses. The EFC is calculated by the federal government based on the student's and family's income, the number of family members, and the number of college students in the family. The college's financial aid administrators calculate the applicant's need for federal student aid from the U.S. Department of Education and other non-federal sources of assistance by subtracting the EFC from the student's *cost of attendance* at a school (COA).

Free Application for Federal Student Aid (FAFSA)

The FAFSA is the financial aid application form parents need to fill out to apply for federal and state student grants, work-study, and loans. The application is available in paper or electronic form and is available in most libraries or by calling FAFSA at (800) 433-3243. You can fill out this application online at http://www.fafsa.ed.gov/ and track the application. You must do two things before completing the FAFSA application. First, you will need to have information similar to your IRS tax returns, so if you have filed a tax return, completing the FAFSA application is easier. Second, you will need to get a U.S. Department of Education PIN number. To obtain your PIN, fill out the brief application at http://www.pin.ed.gov/, and your PIN will be mailed to you in seven to ten days.

FINANCIAL AID, GRANTS, AND LOANS

There are three types of aid: grants and scholarships, loans, and work-study programs. Grants (also called gift aids) do not have to be repaid, and no work is done to repay the money. Grant aid comes from federal and state governments and from individual colleges.

Most scholarships are awarded based on academic merit. However, athletic ability, artistic talent, or plans to enter a particular field of study are bases for receiving some scholarships. *Pell Grants* come through a need-based grant program for undergraduate students. Most Pell grants are given to those with annual family incomes less than $20,000. Eligibility is based on federal EFC.

Most aid is in the form of low-interest loans sponsored by the federal government, which are subsidized by the government. No interest accrues until the student graduates. The Perkins Loan program is a federally subsidized loan with a 5-percent fixed interest rate for undergraduate students and "exceptional" graduate students. The U.S. Department of Education provides the funding to the college, which determines the need. The college combines the funds with some of it's own to allow flexible repayment terms.

Stafford Loans are the most common source of college loan funds. They are fixed-rate, low-interest loans (fixed interest rate—6.8 percent or lower in 2010) available to undergraduate students attending accredited schools at least half time. Stafford Loans are funded by private lenders, but guaranteed by the federal government.

Finally, work-study is a federal program which provides students with part-time employment to help meet their financial needs.

COLLEGE SAVINGS PLANS

Parents use a variety of vehicles to save money for their children's college expenses including bank accounts, U.S. savings bonds, various types of trust accounts, and so-called 529 plans.

Here are some tips for funding higher education.

First, keep a list of all the deadlines for filing applications. Submit the financial aid information as soon as you can after January 1 preceding your child's freshman year in college.

Second, don't give up on expensive private colleges, particularly if you have a gifted child. Private colleges may have the endowments to subsidize gifted students. If the average discount and the percent of undergraduates receiving grants meeting financial need is over 50 percent in both categories, there is a good chance for your child.

Third, both the Perkins and the subsidized Stafford loans (both federal programs) have reasonably low interest rates, and the interest is due only after graduation.

Fourth, avoid borrowing from either a traditional or Roth personal IRA. There are two disadvantages. You will pay taxes on withdrawal from a regular IRA, and the distributions from a Roth IRA may be considered as income for the next year's EFC.

Fifth, retain control of funds in savings plans. Although financial aid may not be an option for high-income earners, financial aid formulas do change over time. Because the current stance on federal aid is that students are expected to be the largest contributors to their educational expense, it may make sense for parents to retain control of the funds placed in 529 plans and prepaid tuition plans.

Sixth, be careful of front-load and high annual fees for plans such as the 529 plans sold by some brokers.

Seventh, keep informed of changes in pension and tax laws. Congress passed the Pension Protection Act of 2006 in August 2006, which was signed by President George W. Bush. The 529 tax permanency provision removes the sunset provision (after 2010) of the tax benefits of 529 plans. The act does not help education savings accounts, which will still face a 2010 sunset of tax benefits.

Taking these steps will ease your planning efforts as you consider higher-education options for your children.

TAKING RISKS

Americans commonly possess an entrepreneurial spirit. Immigrants tend to be comfortable taking only small risk and playing it safe. It is gut-wrenching for parents when an older child wants to switch careers or start a business that involves putting savings at risk or mortgaging a house.

Non-immigrants have the same issue as well but immigrants have grown up in a culture where risks of this sort are simply not taken. We do not burn bridges. How do you reassure your child that it will be fine when you are struggling to understand the reasons for the risk yourself?

Life lessons: Making mistakes, learning from them, and being successful in life is such an American trait that immigrants find it hard to permit their children to follow that path. However, you must have faith in your children's abilities and stop thinking of the time they take to make a decision or to change their mind about their career as a waste.

NOTES

1. Laurie Olsen, *Made in America: Immigrant Students in Our Public Schools* (New York: New Press, 1988).

2. "Asian Nation: Asian American History, Demographics, and Issues," http://www.asian-nation.org/model-minority.shtml.

3. "The Rhodes Trust," http://www.rhodesscholar.org/scholars.

4. Richard E. Nesbitt, *The Geography of Thought: How Asians and Westerners Think Differently—And Why*. (Washington DC: Free Press, 2003).

5. College Board Web site, http://www.collegeboard.com/student/pay/add-it-up/4494.html.

6. Ibid.

Chapter Five

Life Partners

The immigration process and the stress of acculturation will likely stress the parental marriage like nothing a couple has faced before. If the marriage occurred long before immigration, the communication between the couple has probably developed enough that they will grow together.[1] However, if the marriage has occurred in the immediate pre-immigration period, the anxiety and stress may be de-stabilizing enough that marital issues spill over into the raising of the children.

Navigating the difficult territory related to sexuality, love, and marriage between two very disparate cultures is the most stressful of all issues to be faced by immigrants and their children. The open sexuality all around them threatens the beliefs of most immigrant parents. Virginity is expected before marriage and contact between boys and girls may have been limited. As the children come of age, particularly the girls, immigrant parents are often consumed with fear, suspicion, and mistrust and tend to become more authoritative. The fear of unwanted pregnancies in their daughters drives a lot of immigrant parents to clamp down on any contact with boys.

Girls have been shown to have more difficulty adjusting to American life than do boys. This is exhibited by their higher rates of diagnosed depression. They also have the fear of being married off early to a person of their parent's choosing, without completing their education. In order to cope with the pressures at school to fit in, and at home to remain true to their culture, they may resort to lying about their friends, activities, and their socialization with the opposite sex.

The roles of religion and caste are also a major area of conflict in immigrant families. Unlike the openness of religious faith in the U.S. and the right of people to change their religion of birth, most children of immigrants will encounter a strong negative response and often serious consequences, such as being disowned by their families if they change religions.

Some religions require that the couple be of that same faith before they can be married under the rules set by that religion. That means that the other partner has to change his or her religion to marry. Even if one partner changes religions just so the marriage can take place and does not really practice the new faith, the act still creates significant disruption of the parent-child relationship.

Further, although the aspiring couple may share the same religion, parents often expect them to marry within the same caste. Muslim parents may differentiate between lower social class and the Rajput class or between Sunni or Shia sects of Islam. Sikhs may indicate that they prefer a particular region of the Punjab. Hindu parents may advise against inter-marriage with the lower or "scheduled" caste class.

This becomes clear when one looks at any ethnic newspaper. The advertisements on the "Marriage Wanted" page uniformly specify a preference for religion, caste, or sect. It becomes clear from the language in these ads that the parents or relatives are controlling the process. As a result, second-generation adults discretely frequent Web sites catering to a search for partners within immigrant communities. When it comes to marriage, Americanization stops at the front door for a lot of immigrants.

Life lessons: Remember that you are not in your native country. No matter how much you wish that your children follow your footsteps, it is highly unlikely that they will agree to your preferences. You certainly do not want to lose your child over this important issue.

CHOOSING A LIFE PARTNER

Immigrant parents have to understand the changes that have overtaken the institution of marriage in the U.S. Traditional marriage has increased 7 percent while cohabitation has almost doubled.[2] A divorce rate of 4.95 per 1000 people in the U.S. is the highest in the world.[3] The concept of adultery is becoming old fashioned.

Parents immigrating to the U.S. will be faced with this because their children's friends will often come from single-parent homes or from homes where the couple is unmarried. The immigrant parents will have to explain to their children the sanctity of marriage and the seriousness of steps leading to marriage and the commitment to honor and love your spouse. The children need to see you exhibit the honor, love, and fidelity that are important parts of that commitment.

It all starts with respect. The single most important message I have tried to convey to our children about marriage is the importance of respecting your partner. Loss of respect can manifest itself in several ways. It may include speaking ill about your partner in their absence, making dismissive gestures or making faces at them and being sarcastic or putting them down in public. It can also mean belittling their work or occupation, their appearance or physical features, or even comparing the spouse with someone else. When the children observe this behavior, no amount of a display of love and affection can overcome the message of disrespect. This behavior is powerful and corrosive, even if it is rarely exhibited.

Parents who are new immigrants are often shocked by the behavior of parents shown on television. Married couples are shown insulting one another, screaming at each other, and them apologizing and making up. Children watching these shows need to have some context explained to them.

One of my favorite stories I told to my children is about how I married their mother. I was in medical school with marriage the furthest thing from my mind. Back in the late 1960s, boys were generally of a marriageable age by age twenty-two or twenty-three, and girls were expected to be married before they were twenty years old. So, it came as no surprise that my parents started to bring the subject up when I was nineteen years old.

When that did not work for a year, they recruited my maternal grandmother, knowing that I would have a difficult time saying no to her. It was her words that I still remember. She sat me down and said of the woman they had in mind for me, "This girl has character and comes from a very good family." Noticing my blank look, she went on, "Yes, she is also brilliant in her studies and is very pretty also." Her statement emphasized the fact that appearance, although important, is superseded by character, family, and personality, traits that are far more important.

Although much less frequent in large urban areas, an arranged marriage is still a tradition in the Indian sub-continent, as well as in other communities and countries. Marriage is not just between two partners; it also joins both families. Generally this starts with the family "screening" girls deemed suitable for their son, either through viewing photographs or personally. The process is mediated by a religious or social contact or even a family member. This then progresses to the boy meeting several of the top choices before huddling with his parents and announcing their choice.

The girl's side also starts their own investigation through their informal channels before they will agree to meet with the boy. Either way, there are often several meetings which are all semi-arranged, although no chaperone is present these days.

This tradition gives the husband an advantage and dominance early in the marriage. Over time, depending on the two personalities, the relationship evolves, as it does in all marriages, until a happy medium is reached. If the male domination persists by force, the traditional marriage leaves the wife little room to negotiate.

Although some immigrants, especially those coming to the U.S. over a decade ago, have married by arrangement through families, their own relationships change away from their background culture. This is because the women are exposed to more freedom, able to earn a living, and make independent decisions. They are gradually able to assert their important role in the partnership. The relationship may not be equal in every aspect, but it is more balanced than it would have been in their native country.

The children of immigrant parents sometimes have trouble reconciling their mother's role in the family with that they see in their friends' homes or the media. The mother may be seen as more subservient to their father, and some adult children may be resentful of the lack of assertiveness of their mother. Parents need to be sensitive to this and attempt to explain that men and women have equal but different roles within the family. If their mother is less equal in some matters, she is more equal in other matters, over which the father has practically no say whatever.

I have related my grandmother's words as a means of hammering into our children to look beyond outward appearances. I would expect the hormonal rushes to play their part, but hitting the pause button long enough to get to know the family and how the future spouse treats them is very important. The passion fades. What is left is who we really are in our baseline state.

Our son was madly in love with a beautiful girl during his junior year of high school, and within a year was ready to commit to a permanent relationship. There was a slight hitch. She wanted him to convert to her religion. The red flag went up immediately. By that time, I had built enough of a relationship with him that he wanted our approval, without which he would not have proceeded to give his commitment. I explained that anyone who wanted him to change the religion of his birth wanted to alter his relationships with his parents and his entire family. Was he ready to do that? I finally told him "You are too young to understand this right now, but are going to have to trust my judgment on this one and take a pass." He did. It was painful, and as parents, we also suffered with him.

Fortunately, he later met and fell in love with a girl who understood him and shared his dreams. He brought her home several times for us to get to know her. He finally asked our opinion before making his decision. We understood how much our approval meant to him. We also looked at her character, how she dealt with her parents and elders, and how she exhibited the values taught her by her parents. We concluded that his future life partner had the character, the intelligence, and the looks that were gifts from our Creator. Time will tell, but years after we are gone, he will be grateful to his parents for speaking their mind when we disagreed with him.

Life lessons: Trust between you and your children will pay dividends in the area of potential marriage partners. Probably the most you can expect is that the children are agreeable to meeting people you may suggest as possible life partners. Your opinion is very valuable to your children, so use the privilege well. Keep communication channels wide open.

DATING

The period during which their children are dating is a very stressful time, particularly for immigrants. They come with their social views shaped by the fairly conservative norms of their home countries. Immigrant parents assume dating necessarily means indulging in sex.

Another misconception, a holdover from their own culture, is that dating equates with an intention to marry. In most non-western cultures, there is very little intimacy before marriage, including kissing and petting, although in the larger cities the dating routine is no different than it is in the U.S. Immigrants are also used to a monogamous relationship. Some families coming from Muslim countries are very strict and expect their children, without dating, to marry someone the parents have picked. It is amazing that a few children actually agree to go along with this ancient custom. However, for most children, this sets off alarm bells and makes them the butt of jokes. They respond by either lying to their parents about their dating relationships or simply avoid bringing their date's home. Exercising too much control will lead your children to hide things from you.

Immigrant parents want to be involved in their children's social lives and have opinions on whom they date. Children will often grow up hearing parents tell them that they would prefer that the children choose someone in their own culture. This is not to say that most parents would not accept anyone outside our own culture, but simply express a preference. Unfortunately, that may become a problem sometimes because a lot of time is wasted on square pegs being fit into round holes. So, be careful for what you wish for.

I know it is not common practice in the U.S. for parents to have much of a say in their child's choice of a life partner. Most children do ask and would prefer their parent's approval. But, they regard the final decision as their own. That is the way it should be. Parents do not want the responsibility of making such a decision. However, parents should get involved much earlier than a last minute pre-wedding family introduction.

Life lessons: Speak up if you think the partner is not the right one. I understand that we are supposed to let them learn from their mistakes. However, letting them take a serious fall while you stand by and watch is like allowing them to take a pill they are allergic to just to see how bad the reaction might be. Yes, they have to make the final choice but parents have to speak up. If they do not agree, you will still act as a parent and support them. It is fine to express a preference about marrying within the same community, but being obstinate about it or threatening to cut off relationships may backfire.

BRINGING UP SEX

The worst nightmare for immigrant parents is shame for the family if their daughter becomes pregnant or their son fathers a child out of wedlock. The media have reported incidents in which immigrant parents have killed a daughter just for dating without their approval. Sex before marriage is simply not acceptable in most immigrant communities. At least, it is not acceptable for children to let anyone know that they are sexually active.

I don't know many immigrants who have talked to their children about "safe sex" for several reasons. First, they don't expect the children to have sex before marriage. Second, they are too embarrassed to bring the topic up and hope the school is teaching the subject.

All parents approach the issue differently, depending on the child's gender. There is also no question that girls in our culture are treated differently than boys. My daughter has told me that her brother was treated differently, and the double standard bothered her when she was younger. Asian Indian girls are in general less satisfied with the degree of family cohesion because boys are allowed more autonomy.[4] They are pressured to follow traditional gender roles much more than are boys. In this area of concern, I have never apologized for treating our daughter differently.

In our case, I was designated by my wife to have "the talk" with our daughter. We did. I took her for a walk and generally discussed our thoughts about premarital sex.

I never did ask my children about the choices they made. I have a very good idea, but what is the point of asking? If they say they stayed celibate, I would still wonder if they were telling the truth. If they say they did not, they risk their father being disappointed. Why put them in a predicament? I did what I had to do. They will have to live with their decision, not I. However,

I know the answer without having been told. How? Refer to the section on spying on your children.

Life lessons: Informing and educating children about your values regarding sex is your obligation, not the schools. Your moral values may not turn out to be consistent with that of your child's school. It is awkward for most immigrants to bring up the topic, even more than for the parent brought up in a Western culture. At the very least, set expectations and hope for the best.

COHABITATION

Not too long ago, living together or cohabitation was considered immoral and totally unacceptable in most families in the U.S. In the non-westernized world, it is still not acceptable, and indeed adultery is punishable by stoning in a few countries. Attitudes have softened considerably in the U.S., where it is estimated that over 5 million people live together outside of marriage. In a recent report, about 9 percent of males and females between the ages of fifteen and forty-four live together prior to marriage, compared to 40 percent who are married and live together.[5]

That is not to say that these couples do not act married in terms of being faithful to each other and in sharing duties or raising children just like married folks. They just do not have legal marriage status. However, the good news is that about 50 percent of cohabitants are married to each other within three years.[6]

So, how does this arrangement go down with immigrants? Their first reaction on hearing that one of their children plans to cohabit with someone is probably to strangle them on the spot. The next response is, "Who else knows about this?" Their fear is that their immigrant community will learn of it, and the parents will be judged for their child's actions. The implication is that the parents did not bring up their children with proper values. The parents will also be concerned that their child is now tainted, and that marriage within the community will not be possible. That is a certainty if the child is a girl.

If the parents cannot convince their child to rethink the proposed action, they may react in several ways. The reaction may not be as severe as if the child married outside of his or her race or religion. The response will also be more forceful if their daughter declared her choice. The vast majority of immigrants do not take the extreme, violent steps portrayed occasionally in the press. I have known a few parents who forcefully spirited their daughters (always daughters, not boys) out of the country on some pretext to get them away from their boyfriend. I have also known of parents who had their daughter get an abortion quietly and managed to keep it a secret. It is particularly difficult for parents who strongly believe in life and are forced to choose between their belief and a real life situation faced by their child.

Life lessons: Living together among U.S. adults has become more acceptable, whereas it is still looked down upon as "living in sin" in immigrant communities. Some adult children of immigrants are undoubtedly cohabiting without telling their parents. You can certainly educate them about your values and why you think the practice is not acceptable. However, they live in this environment where it has become acceptable. What are your choices? Correct.

HOMOSEXUALITY

Even though homosexuality has existed in ancient cultures for centuries (Alexander the Great, for instance, was rumored to have been a homosexual), and almost every family has homosexuals within their circle, it is simply not talked about. In our social circle growing up, I know there were whispers about certain men who were apparently happily married having relationships with other men. Yet, if a family were to declare openly that their child was a homosexual, it would probably devastate the entire extended family. A Pew research study in 2003 about global attitudes on homosexuality found that people in Africa and the Middle East generally do not accept homosexuality, whereas Latin Americans are accepting, and the American public is about evenly divided. U.S. immigration laws were notable for a question about sexual preference until the U.S. Congress passed the Immigration Act of 1990, which deleted the "sexual deviation" question from the questionnaire so that it could not be used as a basis for denying U.S. entry to homosexuals.

Attitudes of children of immigrants also appear to have changed. In a recent poll many more children of immigrants accepted homosexuality than did their parents.[7]

MARRIAGE OUTSIDE ETHNIC/RACIAL
OR RELIGIOUS BOUNDARIES

Interracial marriages have been legal in the U.S. for many years now, since the U.S. Supreme Court ruled in *Loving v. Virginia* that laws forbidding interracial marriage were unconstitutional.

From 1980 to 2008, there was been a doubling of the number of marriages (6.7 percent to 14.6 percent) between spouses of different race or ethnicity from each other. The Pew study reports that, of all newlyweds in 2008, 9 percent of whites, 16 percent of blacks, 26 percent of Hispanics and 31 percent of Asians married outside their own race or ethnicity.[8]

Marriages between Asians and white Americans are becoming common, particularly between Asian women and Caucasian American males.[9] In 2006, 41 percent of Asian American-born women were registered as having Caucasian husbands, while 50 percent were married to Asian American men.[10] The interracial marriage incidence among Indian Americans was low, with marriage to Caucasian Americans slightly higher for Indian American males. All other major Asian groups had more marriages outside of their ethnic group for women.[11] Among those Asians raised in the U.S., Filipino and Korean men and Chinese, Filipino, and Korean women were the most likely to marry outside their community.[12] Asian Indian men and women were least likely to have a non-Asian Indian wife.

This is possibly the most sensitive area of the relationship between immigrant parents and their children who may have been raised in the U.S. Immigrant parents have grown up with strict taboos against inter-faith marriage. In some parts of the world, these lead to riots. I know of several couples who have had to leave their communities overnight and settle in another country for fear of being harmed.

There are few things that create more serious rifts within immigrant families than a declaration of intent to marry outside the child's own culture. Almost all non-Caucasian immigrants have in some way let their children know when they are growing up about their preference of finding a mate within their own community.

Again the response is related to the gender of their child. First, the parents that view the arrangement from a religious angle will probably react in the harshest manner. They may cut off all communications and support for the child. A worst case scenario is of course a violent act to preserve their honor. The family may kidnap the child through a ruse to get them out of the U.S. As I said, that has to be a very rare act of insanity. I know of a family where a racist attitude on the part of the father has resulted in the daughter for all practical purposes being excluded from her family. As a professional she was getting ready to marry the man of her choice.

There was one serious problem. He was not from the Indian sub-continent. Not only that, he happened to be African -American. If you saw the movie *Mississippi Masala* with Denzel Washington, you will understand to what I am referring. In the movie, Mr. Washington's character falls in love with a beautiful Indian girl. Her parents are first-generation immigrants and are outraged by her decision to date an African American man.

In the family I knew about, the woman's father demanded that she choose between her man and her family. Because of her father's steadfast opposition to her proposed marriage, the daughter decided to abandon any thought of marriage and has declared that she will never marry. She continues to have a live-in arrangement with her boyfriend. I am not sure how this will end. I do know of other second-generation Indians who have married Muslims, Jews, Christians, and people of other races, including African Americans.

Life lessons: There is a gradual but definite shift in the attitude of most immigrant parents towards inter-religious marriage. It starts with being very much closed minded and letting children know very early that they will have to marry someone within their own religion, and indeed within their own sub-caste. Then, as children get into their late twenties, some permissiveness creeps in, and some parents start to accept partners of different faiths. Realize that your child's happiness is not negotiable, is it?

WEDDINGS

So, your children have chosen their life partner and are now ready to get married. Traditions vary by country and faith. Inter-faith weddings are handled usually in one of two ways. There are two separate religious ceremonies or there is a single "Unitarian" marriage or even just a court marriage. We have witnessed many inter-faith weddings involving someone from the Christian or Jewish faith with someone from the Hindu, Muslim, or Buddhist faiths. It is almost always the parents who hold rigid views and create problems. Almost always, the children have talked about the issue and become comfortable with their own decision.

The biggest obstacle in these types of weddings is the issue of one partner converting to another faith. This brings up some serious resistance and some finesse if the conversion is required by one party. Most times, this is because parents do not want to admit to their friends and family that their child was made to convert to another faith. Both sides know, in most but not all cases, that these conversions don't mean anything because the person being converted knows nothing about their new faith and is not likely to practice it. But, saving face is important, and so parents have to come up with a compromise.

The other issue is who pays for the wedding? Generally, Christians and Jewish weddings in the U.S. are fairly small affairs, and the girl's side pays for most of the usual wedding expenses. However, most immigrants are used to large crowds of family and friends and extended celebrations. We have known weddings to cost $500,000. Immigrant communities have differing traditions. In some the boy's side pays for most expenses and in others the girl's side pays for the wedding. It is best to talk to other parents of your community in the U.S. and discreetly enquire about the customary arrangements. Parents and children from both sides then meet and agree on a suitable formula ahead of time and settle after the wedding. If one side has a much larger guest list, they should expect to cover the extra cost.

Lately, I have noticed the girl's and boy's sides sharing expenses equally for the main reception and then paying for their own individual events. The young adults about to be married also cover some of the expenses but not as much as do nonimmigrant children growing up in the U.S. It depends on the financial situation of the parents and the children themselves.

Life lessons: Inter-faith weddings are very touchy, and delicate negotiations are required. Talk of conversion of one party to another faith is a combustible issue. Conversations about sharing expenses and the formula to be followed are best started early.

DIVORCES

According to the U.S. Census Bureau, Asians are less likely to be separated, widowed, or divorced (10 percent compared to 19 percent of the rest of the population). Within various Asian groups, Asian Indians were the most likely to be married (69 percent) and Vietnamese the least likely (56 percent).[13] There is a clear perception among immigrants that a marriage is subject to significantly more stress in the U.S. than in their home countries. The idea of a divorce, though unpleasant for all immigrants, is particularly a stigma for Hindus, where re-marriage, particularly among women, is looked down on. It is more of a cultural roadblock since divorce is legally allowed in all Asian countries.

NOTES

1. Salman Akhtar, *Immigration and Identity: Turmoil, Treatment and Transformation* (Lanham, MD: Jason Aronson, 1999).

2. Richard Taylor, "Why marriage?" *Free Inquiry,* 23.3 (2003): 49-51.

3. "People Statistics: Divorce Rate (Most Recent) by Country," NationMaster. com, http://www.nationmaster.com/graph/peo_div_rat-people-divorce-rate.

4. Y. Moideen, "Family Functioning in Asian Indian Adolescents: The Effects of Acculturation and Gender," (Unpublished Masters diss., DePaul University, Chicago, Il, 1992).

5. "Marriage and Cohabitation in the United States: A Statistical Portrait Based on Cycle 6 (2002) of the National Survey of Family Growth," *Vital and Health Statistics*

23.28 (February 2010), U.S. Department of Health and Human Services, http://www. cdc.gov/nchs/data/series/sr_23/sr23_028.pdf.

6. Ibid.

7. "Children of Immigrants More Gay Positive: Poll," CBC News, May 15, 2009, http://www.cbc.ca/canada/montreal/story/2009/05/15/quebec-homosexuality-poll.html.

8. Jeffrey S. Passel, Wendy Wang, and Paul Taylor, "Marrying Out: One in Seven New U.S. Marriages is Interracial or Interethnic,) Pew Research Center Publications, June 4, 2010, http://pewresearch.org/pubs/1616/american-marriage-interracial-interethnic.

9. "Intimate Relations Between Races More Common Than Thought," University of Michigan News Service, March 23, 2000, http://www.umich.edu/news/index.html?Releases/2000/Mar00/r032300a.

10. "American Families and Living Arrangements: 2006," U.S. Census Bureau, http://www.census.gov/population/www/socdemo/hh-fam/cps2006.html.

11. "Interracial Dating and Marriage," part 1 Asian Nation, http://www.asian-nation.org/interracial.shtml.

12. "Interracial Dating and Marriage," part 2, Asian Nation, http://www.asian-nation.org/interracial2.shtml.

13. "The American Community—Asians: 2004," American Community Survey Reports, U.S. Census Bureau (Feb. 2007), http://www.census.gov/prod/2007pubs/acs-05.pdf.

Chapter Six

Friends and Family

The biggest culture shock for most immigrants from Eastern cultures is the difference in family dynamics. While there is considerable variation within the U.S. with regard to closeness of members of a family unit, the closest unit is still not as cohesive as the average family unit in non-westernized society. Family adaptation and cohesion is seen as a continuum based upon their boundaries, according to Minuchin.[1] Members of the *disengaged* family are the least dependent on each other for support, with little sense of loyalty or belonging.

The other extreme is the enmeshed family, in which members exhibit a strong sense of belonging, loyalty, and interdependence. The third group is somewhere in the middle, where there is still room for individual exploration and problem solving. This continuum changes over time, and adaptation occurs as these families immigrate to where the power structure, roles, and relationships all evolve to varying degrees. It has been noted in ethnographic studies that core values do not change but pragmatic values do change over time.[2] The families may, for example, allow higher education for girls and even some socialization between the sexes but discourage intermarriage with other ethnic groups.

When we came to the U.S., we were missing our vital support system. Gone were parents, aunts, uncles, cousins, brothers, and sisters. For immigrants, friends often take the place of extended family. For the second generation because of distances, siblings and cousins are likely to be a source of support in difficult times. Non-westerners generally look upon cousins as brothers and sisters. Parents of second-generation immigrants should strive to encourage and promote strong relationships between other children of extended family members. We should make it clear that parents are here to support them for a limited time. After we leave this earth, they will have to rely on each other and their extended family for support.

The bonds between our children and our parents (their grandparents) are special albeit short lived in a lot of cases. Unfortunate are children who grow up and have never seen their grandparents or really known them. It is incumbent upon parents to encourage, even vigorously steer, their children towards them. It was a conscious decision for us to take our children as many times as we could to see their grandparents overseas. We barely had enough money to cover the airfare, but we sacrificed elsewhere. Over the years, they have come to know them and their other extended family very well. Our children have taken trips on their own to spend time with their grandparents.

You should encourage them to spend time with grandparents independent of your visits as they get older. My eighty-four-year-old father has his own Facebook social networking page on the Internet (courtesy of our daughter-in-law) and enjoys seeing pictures of all his grandchildren and their friends. He has seen us and his great-grandson via the miracle of technology, the webcam. I hooked it up on one of my trips to visit him.

Life lessons: Teach your children that their extended family and closest friends, no matter how eccentric, will be their support system after their parents are gone. So, they should build solid relationships and make the effort to stay in touch with extended family and friends. Have your children establish an independent relationship with their grandparents.

CHILDREN WATCH HOW YOU TREAT YOUR PARENTS

As a physician who has dealt with children of elderly patients, I have been struck with the variation in how the children treat their needy parents in time of sickness. It is generally believed in Eastern culture that the elderly parents in the West are shunted off to nursing homes while children enjoy an extravagant lifestyle. Popular media portray children in the West visiting their elderly parents once a week in a nursing home. While it is true that, in general, older parents do not stay with their children on a permanent basis, I have seen it enough times to know that generalizations in this regard are not fair.

It is also true that it is common in the Indian sub-continent and other cultures for parents to stay with their children, who take care of them in their golden years. In large cities with limited space in apartment living, it is less frequent than in times past, where residences were large and cheap labor in the form of servants was available to care for the elderly.

Generalities aside, people take responsibility, or choose not to, regardless of which part of the world they are located in. However, I have seen all kinds of families having to deal with sick and dying parents. Because of two-career families and financial constraints, some children maintain a distance in a very formal relationship with their parents. Other children realize their obligations and choose to heavily involve themselves in caring for their parents. I believe a lot of children learn lessons early in life that prepare them for the day they will be asked to choose whether to, and how much to, care for their parents. These lessons are primarily learned by watching how their parents treat their own parents.

My parents are currently living in another continent and time zone. One of the only regrets I have had leaving my country of birth to immigrate to the U.S. is my inability to take care of my parents as they have grown older. As the oldest son, I have felt an obligation to be the main resource for them. I have struggled with my responsibility and have done the best I could, occasionally short changing my own family to travel long distances several times a year to spend time and do various chores for them.

My children have watched my angst and observed the heartache. They have seen the guilt, the effort it has taken, the patience, and the sense of duty that has been at the core of my bond with my parents. I regard my parents as a gift from God. My children see this. They watch as I patiently deal with the 2 a.m. overseas phone calls, listen to the same complaints about my father's back pain, support my mother in any way possible, and prepare for the day I will lose them. There is nothing I can say to my children about what I may need from them as I get older, that can be as powerful as my actions.

A proper parental relationship is described by Dr. Laura Schlesinger in her book *Ten Stupid Things Couples Do to Mess Up Their Relationships* as she relates a story told to her by a rabbi.[3] A great flood occurred, during which the papa bird was caught in a fierce storm with his three baby birds. He was trying to carry each of his babies across a river, one by one, not knowing if he would be able to save all of them. As he carried the first one over he asked the baby bird, "Baby bird, will you take care of me even when you have your own baby birds?" The baby looked at the river below and excitedly replied, "Oh yes! Anytime you need something, I'll be there to take care of you; do not worry, no matter what it takes." The father dropped the bird into the river and flew back for the second bird.

He asked the same question of the second bird, got the same answer, and dropped the bird into the river. When he asked the third baby bird the same question, the bird replied, "I will promise you that I will take care of you the same way you have always taken care of us." The father carried the baby across the river. The lesson she emphasizes is that the best way to honor your parents is to learn how to deal with your parents when you are growing up. You watch your parents' examples, and then apply them.

Second-generation immigrants are now facing the same dilemma their non-immigrant friends are: What to do with their retired parents or parents separated by death. Elderly parents in Asian culture are respected, honored, and taken care of in their old age, whereas in Western culture children respect the independence and desires of their elderly parents. So, the children are caught in a dilemma. Are they expected to insist that their parents come to live with them, even if the parents are reluctant, knowing that, in their parents' culture, this is what is expected of them? Or, should they encourage and assist their parents in residing in a retirement facility? The parents may have concerns about becoming babysitters and caretakers if they agree to move in with their children.

Life lessons: You will probably be treated the same way your children see you treat your parents. So, think about that before you snap at your parents over trivial issues. It is reasonable to discuss issues of retirement ahead of time and give your children a clear idea of your desires if one of you dies. You do not have to have a written document like a living will or a healthcare power of attorney, but your children should know about your wishes ahead of time.

EXTENDED FAMILY

The world is made up of all kinds of people and personalities. So, why should your family be any different? Our family has some real characters, just as other families. Some are not so pleasant or easy to deal with. We have the nay-sayers, the backstabbers, the whiners, the arrogant, and our share of idiots. Yet, they are part of the family, and we bend over backwards to include them on family occasions. There are occasional perceived insults or slights when none are intended, but we still nurture the relationships. You cannot divorce yourself from your relatives. They are part of the fabric of every family.

It is an opportunity for parents to teach tolerance, if you want to look at this as the glass being half full rather than half empty.

My knowledge of palmistry early in life gave me some insight in trying to read people. In medical school I used a roller and ink to collect palm prints of many colleagues so I could later correlate their success in life with the indicators on their palms. Of course my friends accused me of adopting the hobby just so I could hold hands with the girls in my class. As I came across an increasing number of people whose lines did not correlate with indications of illness or disaster, I learned to rely on the art much less to predict future events. Palmistry was helpful in judging people's temperament and character. It did not prevent me many years later from asking to see a financial advisor's hands as I was deciding whether to trust him with my money. I did. He did not turn out to be a particularly astute advisor, although he was not a cheat or a liar.

"A friend may well be reckoned the masterpiece of nature," according to Ralph Waldo Emerson. For immigrants, friends often are the only resource available to fill the void left by the absence of parents, siblings, and extended family. In our case, they have more than filled in as "uncles" and "aunties" for our children. The children got to know each and every uncle and aunty and learned to interact with them as family. The children went with us to graduations, marriages, and deaths. Now that our children are older, they still meet our friends with great affection and show up for major events that occur in our friends' lives. We are confident that these aunties and uncles, and in many cases their children, will be resources for our children, and they will in turn reciprocate.

In an interesting twist, I had a close friend tell me recently that he was disappointed with his cousins recently when he flew all the way coast to coast to visit his sister for the weekend. It seems that my friend's cousins knew well ahead of time that he would be coming. The cousins lived less than an hour away but said they could not come to meet him for what seemed to my friend to be fairly weak excuses. I related this to our son in passing. He immediately responded with, "Dad, if I ever do anything like that would you please slap me." That got my attention. I was very proud that all the work we had done to instill in him the value of being with family had borne fruit.

Good friends and acquaintances are two very different things. Most people we call friends are just acquaintances. We meet them occasionally, most often at other people's houses, and remember their names and faces. Conversations restart on the same note they ended on the last time you met, and you end up not knowing anything more at this meeting that you did the last time. Can you remember the names of their children? Do you know about their last serious illness? Will they leave everything to come to help you when you ask? Will they keep your secret safe? Do you never expect them to say things behind your back? Probably not. That means they are acquaintances only.

Good friends are rare commodities to be treasured. Children need to be exposed to these treasures while you are collecting and savoring these friends. Nurturing a friendship is often labor intensive. Trust between friends takes a long time to develop. It takes frequent interactions and consistency to allow trust to grow. Hidden agendas will reveal themselves over time. When they come to the forefront, all the previous hard work to establish trust is wasted.

There are about six families that have become like family members and more than friends for over thirty years. We have been through births, deaths of family, marriages, divorces of a few of their children, anniversaries, health issues, and recently celebration of our sixtieth birthdays. There are differences in our origins and our professions, our political views from far left to conservative and personalities ranging from the neurotic to passive aggressive, but we have stuck together because we know each other well enough to know that we can rely on each other completely. Our children have seen these relationships and admire the support we give each other. We treat each other's children like our own. We have all tried to have all of our children relate to one another in similar ways. That does not work. They are different people, so after a few attempts, we accepted the fact that they would stay acquaintances, not friends. However, the value of these friendships is incalculable. When the parents are no longer living, our children will run into each other, as they surely will, and the old bonds will surface.

The importance of standing by your friends during tough times cannot be over emphasized. The loss of a two-year-old son, the suicide of an adult child, a nasty divorce, and financial difficulties are all circumstances we have shared with each other. One of my best friends from medical school has been a life long friend. I have experienced his joys and tragedies right along with him and his family. After forty years of a comfortable exchange of greetings, meetings, children's marriages, and the like, he developed colon cancer with spread to his liver. I flew to Houston, where he had a major liver operation, to be with him and his family. Then I saw him once a year in India while he battled his cancer, and we talked on the phone once a week. Finally, it appeared he was near the end, and I made the decision to fly to Bombay, India, to see him before he died. I made it just in time, spending three priceless days with him, his wife, and grandchildren. Two days after I left, he quietly passed away. My children saw the interaction and learned the value of standing by your friends during periods in life when any support is truly welcomed. He was not a brother by birth, but some relationships go much deeper.

The children also need to see how far you will go to help your friends and even their children. The "uncles" and "aunties" they see often growing up are also a great resource later as the children grow up and need help with everything from letters for admissions committees to serving as references for jobs. I have taken a particular interest in helping our friend's children success by helping them develop their résumés for admission to medical school. They have been well served as I have gotten them research positions or hired them as research associates and taught them basic research methods so that by the time they finished they would have some publications to their credit. I feel great pride in the small role I have played in their professional success.

Life lessons: The value of good friends needs to be demonstrated to children. Be there for your friends if you expect them to be at your side when you need them. Loyalty to friends must be shown by walking the walk. Bad mouthing them behind their backs while appearing to be the best of friends to their face is setting a bad example. Do not try too hard to force your children to follow in your footsteps in choosing who their friends will be. However, the argument that your friends will be useful in their career advancement may get your children's attention.

GIVE AND TAKE

Friends are generally considered to be a source of great comfort, support, and joy. Sometimes they can be life savers. One incident really stands out. While in high school, our daughter was talking on the phone to her girl friend one evening, as she often did, when the phone line suddenly went dead. Most people would have given up after a few attempts and assumed that the other phone line was simply defective. But she persisted because her instincts told her something serious was wrong. She finally traced a family member and asked them to go check on her in the bathtub, from where her friend happened to be calling. Minutes later, the family called the paramedics because they found the girl unconscious in the bathtub following a seizure. She survived and we still get Christmas cards from the girl's family.

However, friends can be, and often are, a source of pain. It always seems like I gave more to my friends than I received. A lot of people I talk to relate the same feeling of a lack of reciprocity with close friends. Our son also related on several occasions that some of those he regarded as his best friends did not reciprocate his compulsion to do all he could for them when they were in need. I made an effort to relate similar experiences, in which friends, sometimes unknowingly, ended up hurting feelings. I encouraged him to not let this negative experience discourage him from trying to form close friendships. It is a difficult process to teach children to shift from a perspective that is self-centered to one that embraces other viewpoints. Just learning to keep quiet and listen to others is a difficult task for some children. Parents have to lead the way in teaching their children how to deal with the differences between friends, even when those friends do not meet expectations.

Life lessons: It does not matter how much you care about your friends, some of them will not care back to the same degree or in the same way. They may be putting all they have into the relationship, but that may not be up to your standards. Teach your children not to be disappointed at small setbacks and not to necessarily expect to receive the same effort they put into the relationship.

STABILITY AT HOME

While they were growing up, most of our children's friends were from broken homes. Our children told us that, throughout school and college, their friends reminded them how lucky they both were to have two parents at home. Our children took that for granted and came to find out through their friends how unusual a two-parent home was. Our daughter wrote us a card several weeks after she left for college, in which she came out for the first time to thank us for providing her with a stable home to grow up in. She said she took it for granted and assumed all other kids had the same environment. They did not carry the burden of worrying about whether their parents would be together while they were growing up.

It is hard enough to go through the normal teenage experience without being in the middle of parental discord.

NOTES

1. Salvador Minuchin, *Families and Family Therapy* (Cambridge, Mass: Harvard University Press, 1974). See also Salvador Minuchin and H. Charles Fishman, *Family Therapy Techniques* (Cambridge, Mass: Harvard University Press, 1981).

2. S. P. Wakil, C. M. Siddique, and F. A. Wakil, "Between Two Cultures: A Study in Socialization of Children Immigrants," *Journal of Marriage and the Family* 43 (1981): 929-940.

3. Laura C. Schlessinger, *Ten Stupid Things Couples Do to Mess Up Their Relationship* (New York: Harper, 2002).

Chapter Seven

Faith

In a 2007 poll of 1003 adults, the Gallup organization published the results of a U.S. survey about belief in God. Ninety percent of those polled said they believed in God or a universal spirit and 81 percent believed in the concept of heaven.[1] The percentage who believe in a higher power has decreased by 4 percentage points between 2001 and 2007, with a corresponding increase in those not believing. In a similar survey of 1017 adults in 2008, it was observed that "those with a post-graduate degree are the most likely not to believe in God or a universal spirit (9%) while those a high-school degree or less are less likely (5%) to do so."[2]

Richard Lynn, emeritus professor of psychology at Ulster University, has stated that people with higher IQs are much less likely to believe in God.[3] He also observed that religious belief had declined across 137 developed nations in the twentieth century, and this occurred "at the same time as people became more intelligent." Does that mean that we discourage our children from earning their PhD's?

RELIGIONS OF ASIA

Since my background is Asian, a few words of the common religions of Asia.

The three most well known religions in Asia are Hinduism, Jainism, and Buddhism. Islam followed much later. Hinduism had no one single founder. Jainism was founded by Mahavira, and Buddhism by Buddha around 600 B.C. Islam came into the Asia after the death of the Prophet Muhammad (Peace Be Upon Him) around the seventh century C.E. Sufi orders were an off shoot of Sunni Muslims, which were more into the mystical parts of the religion. Guru Nanak, in the fifteenth century, founded Sikhism as a separate faith that was later propagated by nine more gurus.

Over the centuries, various traditions and customs have been shared and morphed to the point that although the faiths are separate, the cultural aspects overlap considerably. Christianity followed the arrival of the Portuguese, Dutch, French, Danish, and finally the British at the end of the fifteenth century.

In China, orthodox religion historically has been a mixture of Confucianism and the worship of ancestors. Later Taoism was replaced by Buddhism at about the same time that Romans were being introduced to Christianity. In Japan, ancestor worship gradually led to Shintoism, which was a combination of ancestor and emperor worship, until Buddhism came in the early part of the sixth century.

Asian immigration has brought new religions to the United States. Although, Hinduism, Islam, and Buddhism are all old religions in Asia, they are relatively new to the U.S. These religions have co-existed for centuries, albeit with some conflicts. The early immigrants settling on the West Coast became assimilated with local communities, including intermarriage with Hispanic Christians.

MY BEGINNING

As a six-to-seven-year-old, I was sick often. Even before that, I remember going to a doctor's office that looked like a garage and getting a shot in each hip every day for weeks. My mother says it was typhoid and adds that I was a very sick kid. At age three, I developed a high fever that would not come down, and the doctors apparently gave up on me. She relates that my "nani" or maternal grandmother, moved by my mothers' despair, took me and put me in Guru-ji's lap with a remark that I was in his hands. (*Guru* is a Sanskrit word for teacher although it generally refers to spiritual teacher. *Ji* is appended to someone's name as a mark of respect, hence, Guru-ji). I got better. My maternal relatives were followers of Sufism. A. J. Arberry defines Sufism as "the mystical movement of an uncompromising Monotheism."[4]

Other religious experts also weigh in on describing Sufism in various ways. Karen Armstrong opines, "Unlike dogmatic religion, which lends itself to sectarian disputes, mysticism often claims that there are as many roads to God as people. Sufism in particular would evolve an outstanding appreciation of the faith of others."[5] According to S. A. A. Rizvi, Shaikh Abdul Rehman Chisti (1683) the Sufi interpreter of the *Bhagawad Gita*, the holy book of Hinduism, remarks that the central part of Krishna's teaching is illustrated in this verse: "O Arjuna whatever you do consider Him as Its author associate none with them and Be assured that all is He that is one and no partner."[6]

My remembrance of Guru-ji is all in Karachi. He sat outside on the lawn in the bright sun, usually with his sunglasses on. He would smoke a hookah often, and it would be shared with others. I remember his voice. He would punctuate his remarks very often with "huuuuu" which is referring to "Him" or God. He would rarely talk about anything but God, although I can remember him laughing occasionally at something funny. I was in the upstairs bathroom where my grandparents lived, my maternal grandmother knocked on the door. She shouted through the door "Are you coming out soon? Guru-ji is giving Zikr (also pronounced *Dikr* also called Mantra or Naam) to all the older kids. I'll try for you if you come quickly." I wrapped a towel around my waist and with wet hair and no shirt came running out with her, down the steps to the large family room where he slept.

Guru-ji was seated on a carpet on the floor with two of my older cousins praying near him. Nani said "Guru-ji, can you give him Zikr also?' He chuckled and then looked at me intently, surveying a small, disheveled squirt (I was short for my age). This was probably early 1958, and I was ten years old. He then said, "He is too young." Nani shot back quickly with, "Guru-ji, he is grown up for his age and understands."

Guru-ji then laughed, looked me over again and slowly motioned me over. I crawled on my knees to where He was sitting. He talked to me and explained the words and how to say them and how to breathe. He asked if I understood. I said yes. He then asked me to practice next to the other kids. We probably sat for a few minutes. Then, he said to go sit every morning and evening. All of us were going to the roof of the large house and sat and practiced every day.

Every morning and evening he sat either outside on the lawn or inside in the family room. The place was full. As soon as he was ready, everyone hurried to sit and listen. Visitors were frequent. It was a heady feeling to have a mantra to recite and be able to sit like the adults and pray. I am sure I did not understand the significance or the power of the Zikr and the importance it was to have on the rest of my life.

Zikr is remembrance through repetition of God's name. Perception of the truth is the object of all meditation and is known by various names in different religions. The Hindu religion calls it nirvana, some Christians call it the via illuminativa and the Sufis call it maarifa. Zikr is done silently (khafi) or loudly (jali). The Sufi finds great pleasure in repeating God's name, as there cannot be any ritual dearer for lovers than constant repetition of the beloved's name.

Finally, murshid or guru is the name of a spiritual guide and mureed or Sheesh or Chela are names for the disciple.

FAITH, RELIGION AND IMMIGRANT YOUTH

Children of immigrant families not born in the U.S. often are confused and conflicted about every part of their existence. They do not understand or fully accept their parents' culture or religion, yet are not ready to accept American culture either. They look different than their peers in school but want to belong and do not wish to stand out in any way. Their parents want them to comply with their native religious and cultural norms, yet do not want to restrict them too much for fear their children might be ostracized in school or the neighborhood. A lot of parents give their children basic instruction in their faith and then hope that the children will turn inquisitive and gradually come to the faith of their family.

There are several reasons why there is a disconnect between immigrant parents and their children who are raised in the U.S. First, the older generation tries to retain control over any structure inherent in the temple, mosque, or church. The young adult may find it difficult to challenge adults and simply takes the easy route by not attending any services. Second, the immigrant youth may see the form of faith practiced at home or in the place of worship as too rigid and rooted in ancient history to be of any relevance to them. This feeling of irrelevance may be reinforced by aged priests or office bearers at the place of worship. Third, the younger immigrants feel uncomfortable in their dress or unable to comply with very specific requirements for attendance at places of worship.

Fourth, the younger immigrants also may not speak or understand the rituals or scripture language and feel out of place when their parents converse in their native language. All it takes is one comment by an older friend of the family about the child's dress, language, or accent to drive the young child away.

Life lessons: Your faith or religion came with you when you arrived in the U.S. Your children, if born here, are being asked to accept something at face value. Take your time with them and teach them without forcing them into anything.

IS FAITH BLIND?

As I have explained, children growing up in the U.S. are encouraged to ask a lot of questions. Religion and your faith will not be an exception. You may have been perfectly fine with blind faith as your parents indoctrinated you into whatever faith you were brought up in. To explain the importance of faith my Guru-ji related a story about a king and his queen who went for a walk on the beach and found one fakir building castles from the sand. A fakir is a person who has renounced worldly desires and devoted himself or herself to a search for God. The queen went up to him and asked him what he was doing. He replied, "I am building castles that are going to be in heaven." The astounded queen asked him if he was willing to sell to her one of his heavenly castles.

The man said that he was building the castles so he could sell them. The queen pointed to the biggest sand castle and asked him for its price. "Five rupees," said the Fakir. The queen immediately gave him the money and recounted the whole episode to the king. The king said, "How stupid you are. The poor man has just duped you of five rupees, and he must be really having a good laugh at your gullible nature." The Queen became a little saddened at what her husband told her.

They returned to their palace and went to sleep. The king dreamed that he was in a wonderful land where he saw fabulous castles, all studded with priceless jewels. Suddenly, he was attracted to a huge, glorious castle, the likes of which he had never seen before. He advanced toward it but was stopped from entering by the guard posted there. To his utter amazement, he saw that the nameplate on the door to the castle and it had his wife's name on it. "This castle belongs to my wife, and surely I have the right to enter it," he told the sentry. The sentry curtly told him that only his wife was allowed to enter, as it belonged to her.

At this point, the king woke up with a start and was quite unhappy with the experience of his dream. The whole day the king was fretting and fuming and as evening approached, he cajoled his queen to accompany him for a walk on the beach. To his great satisfaction, he saw the same fakir building the heavenly castles. Quickly he ran towards him and asked him if he would sell him one of his castles. "Surely," said the fakir, and the king pointed to a tiny castle. "The price for this one will be one-half of your kingdom," said the fakir nonchalantly.

The shocked king protested and told him "But yesterday you sold a very large castle to my wife for only five rupees!"

"I sure did" said the fakir. "Your wife had total, blind faith in what I told her, and she believed me. You, my friend, actually mocked her and made fun of her. You were only convinced that these were real heavenly castles after the lovely dream that you had last night. You needed some proof before you actually believed me."

Telling them similar stories over time may put them in a frame of mind to at least listen to your explanations about your faith.

Life lessons: The point of this tale is that faith in a religion or spiritual being is often blind. A person looking for a spiritual guide must spend a lot of time searching for the true and genuine article among all the frauds that exist today. Children raised in the U.S. usually do not have grandparents or elderly aunts and uncles to tell them about their personal experiences with their faith. They do not grow up listening to stories and experiences that reinforce their faith. Therefore, they are searching for proof that the religion or faith of the parents is genuine and worth their allegiance. Parents may have grown up accepting these tales or personal experiences, but the second generation should not be expected to follow blindly. Let them search on their own terms but continue to tell them of your faith and clearly lay out the principles.

THE ROLE OF PRAYER

Most major religions point to an end of the world as we know it at some undefined time. The paucity of highly spiritual souls sent to uplift humanity by God is given as proof that human existence is coming to an end. Muslims believe that the twelfth and last prophet or Imam Mahdi will arrive on earth before judgment day and rid the earth of injustice and, with Jesus Christ, will battle the antichrist. In Christianity the second coming of Jesus Christ as returning from heaven to earth is promised. In Hinduism, the fourth or last yug (cycle of time) is called Kal Yug. In the spiritual evolution of mankind, Sat Yug, Treta Yug, and Dwapar Yug are followed by Kal Yug, after which the entire cycle is supposed to repeat. The end of the world is presaged by Kal-Yug, during which crime rates will soar, human beings will resort to acting like animals, and wars will be fought leading to destruction.

In view of the pain and suffering associated with human existence, most of us are desperate for comfort and the peace that comes with acceptance of God's will. In Sufism, this is called amur, which implies that one has no choice but to accept God's will. This may be one of the most common questions asked by your children. Can prayer change any outcome? Will asking God make a difference? Although, the era of miracles seems to be waning, that does not mean prayer cannot change the course of events. Sufism teaches that praying for a change in one's destiny is not proper.

If I develop terminal cancer, I should not pray or ask my guru or a similar holy person for the cancer to completely disappear. That is trying to change one's taqdeer or destiny. We are taught that, even though prayer and one's Guru can change destiny in some cases, this often has unintended consequences. For instance, how do I know that my cancer may be cured but my loved ones such as one of my children will not get a similar illness? What is proper is to ask that God give me strength to deal with the cancer, ameliorate my pain and suffering, give me time to enjoy some extra time with my family and put my affairs in order.

I was finishing writing a book about the business of medicine for physicians. At the tail end I came upon a software program that was being used at universities to detect plagiarism by matching student papers with other similar works available on the Internet. I decided to test the software by running several scientific papers I had written, going back ten years. On matching these papers I found several instances where a couple of lines were not placed in quotes or referenced appropriately. I panicked at the thought of being tarred and feathered for plagiarizing. I could not sleep or eat for two days. I prayed like never before, in fear for my reputation.

At about the same time, our son had been without a job for several months. My wife became very disturbed and had trouble sleeping because of what the unemployment was doing to our son. She started to pray very hard. Both of these events were going on at about the same time. One morning she described to me what she had dreamed the night before. Both issues were resolved in a short time. Something that could have turned into an ugly incident went away with hardly a whimper. I also called our son and told him that his luck would change and not to worry. Within a few days, he got several calls for interviews and had his pick of jobs. Luck or divine intervention? I choose to believe our faith and prayer may have altered the outcome.

Most often, though, in my professional life, I have used prayer to ask for God's mercy on sick patients. A few years ago, I had been scheduled to deliver grand rounds (a teaching lecture delivered to staff, residents, and students) at the local university for several months. On that morning, just as I was preparing to leave my hospital, I got called to the emergency room to see a patient who had symptoms of an expanding abdominal aortic aneurysm. An aneurysm is a weakened, ballooned artery in the stomach that could rupture with imminent death. In this case, the pain was from expansion of the artery, although there was no actual rupture or leakage of blood. I thought I had time to deliver the lecture and return to operate on him. The senior resident (trainee physician) assigned to me also came to hear my talk.

However, as soon as we reached the lecture hall, which was about a fifteen-minute drive from the hospital, some instinct prompted me to turn to the resident and ask him to leave immediately and return back to be with the patient. He resisted but acquiesced when I insisted. Half way through the lecture my pager went off and I knew what had happened. I finished quickly and ran to my car. I drove like a maniac through downtown Columbus, Ohio. I prayed hard and begged the Lord and my Guru-ji to be with the patient and not punish him for my actions.

I arrived to find the resident I had sent back to the hospital in control in the operating room with a clamp on the patient's abdominal aorta, the main blood vessel. It had burst in the emergency room while I was giving my lecture. The patient's blood pressure had dropped to zero. The resident had rushed him to the operating room, placed a clamp on the aorta, and then waited for me to arrive. I fixed the leak, replaced the blood vessel with an artificial artery, and the patient recovered uneventfully. I told the patient the story at his first postoperative visit and was grateful that he beat the odds for whatever reason. He flew in from Florida after retirement to visit me annually and thank me for saving his life.

Yes, miracles do happen. But, do I believe that God had listened to my prayers that day and saved my patient's life? Yes, I do. I relate these and many other examples to my children at every opportunity.

Life lessons: Faith does not necessarily come by reading religious texts or attending religious services. Plant the seed early in life and let your children see you practice your faith. One has to be careful not to be overly moralistic and unwilling to consider other people's point of view. Criticizing other religions or faiths will not help your cause with your children.

NO GUARANTEES

When everything is going great, it is easy to get lulled into thinking that you deserve all of the happiness that seems to be yours. You start to assume that this transient phase will last forever and that smooth sailing is guaranteed. Of course, underneath the exterior, the fear lingers that fortunes will turn at some point. And they do in most cases.

It is important that immigrant parents pass on their cultural attitudes, related to how they were taught to deal with adversity. What I tell my children is that happiness was not guaranteed at birth. When bad days come, as they surely will, tell yourself, "This too shall pass." Our son decided to talk to our family's spiritual leader about following in the family's footsteps. During the question and answer private session, the issue came up of how having faith in God and meditation helps in dealing with the curve balls thrown at us during our lives. The answer he was given is that your life is like a small boat in the sea and is being rocked during a storm. Faith and meditation do not prevent the storm but help steady the boat quicker. Faith does not mean you are not susceptible to the thousand cuts and the pain that comes from being alive. It means that the same God that put those obstacles in your way also gave you the strength to deal with the pain. Putting your trust in God is easier said than done, especially when the mind is going over and over the worst case scenario at 200 miles an hour.

Most major events in our lives are not under our control, and to some extent, the often-heard phrase, "I want to take control of my life" seems like a misnomer. What most people probably mean is "I am now going to do what I should have been doing. "That is not the same thing as being in control of one's life. Or they mean, "I want to take control of myself."

That is a life lesson worth teaching your children. The only way to take control of events or your life is paradoxically to leave them in God's hands. If you do, a lot or your worries are lessened, and then you can worry about how you will react and deal with your life or the events that happen. Immigrants come to the U.S. expecting to work hard and become successful. But, most of them also have some degree of fatalism and realize that they can try their utmost, and yet if something is not meant to be, it will not.

Life lessons: Children need to observe how you deal with the obstacles in life and if you walk the walk when you speak about your faith. They need to know that life does not come with any guarantees. Emphasize that faith and meditation help steady the boat of life. Have them watch you demonstrate patience during times of difficulty and give thanks during times of plenty.

BELIEVE THAT YOU WILL BE
JUDGED ON HOW YOU LIVED YOUR LIFE

As immigrants, we are all trying to teach our children to do the right thing. "Why?" they will ask. Most likely your answer will be that they will be judged by how they lived their life on earth. Whatever faith you choose to believe in, almost all of them declare that your actions and deeds will be judged when you leave this life. There are differences among various religions on whether the soul is reincarnated. Regardless, it is critical to tell our children that our deeds are subject to review by a higher authority, even when no one appears to be watching.

As a physician I have had a chance to observe a variety of behaviors among my peers over thirty years. A small minority of physicians are dishonest. As president of the medical staff at a large hospital, I dealt with disciplinary issues among physicians. My impression of the few dishonest physicians I have known is that they are no different in rationalizing their actions than are unsavory characters in the business or political world. Some of the ones I have met were even outwardly religious. However, what I have never understood is how such people square their faith, whatever it was, with their dishonest behavior. If one believes in being judged when you die, then you have to comprehend that actions that hurt other human beings have to be recorded as negative events that will have consequences.

I can honestly say that in my thirty years of medical practice, I have never intentionally done anything to harm my patients or take financial advantage of them. There was one instance in which I should have been more truthful when a patient suffered harm by a trainee. In that case I was strongly advised by my professional liability insurance company not to reveal any information. Detractors talk about conflicts of interest when physicians refer patients for tests in circumstances where they have ownership interest. I found that to be a rather odd claim in most cases. Everything that physicians do has the potential to be a conflict of interest. But, if you truly believe in the concept of judgment, you are not likely to take any steps that will hurt patients or take advantage of them. This concept is an important one for children to learn in almost all faiths.

Faith in the Creator and being judged at some point should make it practically impossible to purposely harm or cheat another human being. Denial and rationalization can mist up the mirror you look at every morning. Greed, a feeling of self-entitlement and an intense focus on keeping up with the Joneses, creates a powerful gravitational pull. The message that we must live according to moral standards needs to be heard loud and clear while children are growing up. Of course, they are watching your actions too. Life lessons are taught over time, repeatedly and by walking the walk.

Life lessons: One should consider God to be in every part of your life and witness to every action or deed that you are part of. When you actually practice this and believe it, you will not try to do something that hurts another human being. You will not try cheating or lying in order to hurt someone. You either will not be able to do it, or if you do, you will have buried that voice really deep. The voice will re surface. Again and again, children need to have their consciences nurtured.

DEATH

"Those who remember me at the time of death will come to me. Do not doubt this. Whatever occupies the mind at the time of death determines the destination of the dying; always they will tend toward that state of being. Therefore, remember me at all times and fight on. With your heart and mind intent on me, you will surely come to me." (*Bhagavad-Gita*)

There are distinct differences in the way various cultures deal with the certainty of death. In general, Western cultures, in my opinion, do not bring children up with reminders of the end of life. The subject is considered to be morbid. In my upbringing there were constant references to death.

However, once death of a loved one occurs, I have been struck with the differences between my background culture and that of the U.S. In funeral services in the U.S. there is often a celebration of the life of the departed family member, with a positive atmosphere surrounding the gathering of family and friends. In most cases, the body is laid out for public viewing. Conversation is the norm. Food is served. Laughter is heard. This eases the family into accepting death. In my culture, the cremation is generally more private, with a lot of rituals that help the family come to peace with the end of life. At home, the family is fairly captive to receiving visitors for many hours each day for twelve days. There is often a lot of crying and ritual wailing by visitors, who expect to be served food and tea for days after the funeral.

I have encouraged discussion of death without being dramatic or morbid about it. For example, I have told my children for several years that I have all the necessary documents, such as my will and power of healthcare attorney in place. I wrote my death instructions many years ago, and they are in a sealed envelope with my first-born. My wife knows exactly where my financial information is kept and the password for the electronic file. There are detailed instructions that include a list of all the advisors, attorneys, and accountants to call at the time of my death.

The point is that, although it will certainly be a traumatic event for my family, the fact that I have been ready for the predictable end is something that I hope makes us value our time together even more. It also reinforces the idea that not talking about it does not postpone the end of life. One day my Guru-ji was sitting watching two kabootars (pigeons) play on the verandah. Suddenly, a cat sprang up and grabbed one of the kabootars and ran off. Guru-ji tried to scare the birds away to no avail. He then remarked, "Death will be like this. No amount of noise or pleading will scare it away."

Another message to be delivered is that it is not death that is to be feared but what happens after death. Khalil Gibran, in his book *The Prophet*, properly puts the fear of death into perspective:

> Your fear of death is but the trembling of the shepherd when he stands before the king whose hand is to be laid upon him in honor. Is the shepherd not joyful beneath his trembling, that he shall wear the mark of the king? Yet is he not more mindful of his trembling? For what is it to die but to stand naked in the wind and to melt into the sun? And what is it to cease breathing, but to free the breath from its restless tides that it may rise and expand and seek God unencumbered?[7]

Indeed, the fear of being judged after death is a blessing, according to Sufism, and is a form of prayer. On the one hand, one should look forward to being one with the Creator and his or her guru. On the other hand, being judged for how you lived your life makes one fearful of hurting another individual, whether it involves a crime, cheating, lying in order to hurt another person, or simply not remembering God.

Life lessons: Talk about death with your children in a normal, casual way, as you would the next phase of your career. Let them understand that life is indeed short and emphasize that every bit of time spent together is precious. Have them understand that this journey will end. Are they prepared for the next phase? We prepare for the next phase of our careers. It seems to me that preparation for the phase after this life should be even more important. The consequences of their acts should be discussed relative to the after life.

WHAT ARE YOU HERE FOR?

As children get older and creep into their teen years, they begin to ask questions about why we exist and why they were born into your family. Like most of us, they often wonder about our purpose for being here on this planet. Philosophers and religious scholars have long pondered this question. It is fair to say that since no one has returned from that other world to inform us, we just do not know the answer. There is an explanation that was told to me that shines some light on this question and may help you explain things to your children.

Guru-ji illustrated how we are duty bound to think about and remember God at all times. When He made man, He was categorically assured that we would always remember Him. When a woman conceives, the fetus grows in her womb. It undergoes a lot of "suffering," as it is hung upside down in the totally dark confines of the stomach, within all the body fluids. Out of sheer frustration, the fetus calls out to Him, "Please release me from this torture." The Lord says "If I release you from this torture chamber, what will you do?" "I promise I will always remember you and never, ever will I forget you." The Good Lord listens to the pleas and feels sorry, and finally He puts an end to all the baby's miseries, and the baby comes out into this world. The moment the child sees the brightness all around and finds itself in a most wonderful surrounding, with all the fussing and the adulation being showered by everyone around, the baby forgets the promise made to God.

One of the few regrets I have had in immigrating to this great country is my limitation in instilling this faith into my children. From talking to other immigrants, this is a common feeling. I believe I have succeeded to some extent, in that they believe strongly in a divine power and have turned out to be great human beings. I think it takes all the effort a parent can give to convincing young children that there is more to this life then the next hot music album, a newly released video game, or even the next test. It is not easy to put success and failures during school years in the proper context because of the necessary emphasis on grades.

In my case, what helped me was what my parents did for me. They turned me on to their spiritual guide. I learned to appreciate the proper role of my Guru-ji as my life progressed specially in difficult times, away from my parents and extended family, all alone in a foreign country with little support.

Why is a Guru-ji important? My Guru-ji related the story of an eagle that was sharing some food with another bird in a ditch. While they were feeding, a spider came along and spun a web around them both. The eagle suddenly saw the web and assumed that some hunter had thrown a net around them to keep them from escaping. The eagle quietly became resigned to its fate and sat still. Another eagle flew by, watched the two birds sitting still and asked the eagle what the problem was. The first eagle said he was waiting for the hunter to show up as he was trapped. The second eagle urged the first to spread its wings and make an effort to get out. The first eagle tried and was able to fly away.

The analogy is that we, like the eagle, are trapped in the everyday world, the spider web, and need to make a spiritual effort ourselves and or either with the assistance of a guru or second eagle to free ourselves from the entanglements around us.

Life lessons: Keep all of your children's achievements in perspective. Let them see you handle life's hard knocks with grace and verbalizing a greater purpose in our being on this earth. Try very hard to find them a spiritual guide, whether it is a preacher, priest, rabbi, or someone else wise enough to answer questions in a forthright manner. Encourage them to keep in close touch with their guide throughout their lives.

PRAYER

Most families lead their children to participate in some sort of ritual associated with their religion. This may be saying grace at the dining table, going to once-a-week services at a temple or church, or taking a class meant to teach a religious text. Other than the rituals, the majority of us remember prayer when we are faced with the usual roadblocks in life. How many thank God when things are going well? When was the last time you expressed gratitude at a great meal, a long awaited family reunion, a relaxing hot shower, lovemaking? Were you thankful if you had enough money to take a trip around the world?

Children observe us calling on God when we have a crisis on our hands. No crisis, no prayer. In Sufism, thankfulness or shukr when all is well is a form of prayer. Prayer does not have to be restricted to fixed times in the morning, evening, or on Sunday mornings. One is breathing twenty times a minute during waking hours. So, why can we not pray during the day while we are at work, showering, driving, or simply relaxing?

There are plenty of lessons to be taught here. One time most of my siblings and I were in a car that rolled over twice, and all escaped unhurt. We were driving to a spiritual place, and were convinced that we escaped because of the destination.

Do you believe prayer can change the course of events? If you do, do your children believe, too? As a physician I have witnessed that plenty of families pray for a miracle. In a recent study of trauma patients, 57 percent of the public believed that divine intervention could save a person when their physician had pronounced their condition futile. Sadly, according to the study, only about 20 percent of the healthcare givers surveyed believed in divine intervention.[8] All religious texts have examples of divine intervention in the form of miracles, which changed the course of humankind.

Life lessons: Practice your faith and be sure to educate your children in whatever daily rituals are involved, whether it is saying prayers at meal time or praying several times a day. Be prepared for a time when they make excuses because they do not want to join in. Persuasion, without being confrontational, takes patience. Make persistent attempts to explain why they are likely to need their faith during their life.

SCHOOL AND PRAYER

Immigrants need to understand a little bit about the controversy related to prayer in school. School systems in the U.S. follow the separation of church and state principle, which is said to be 'inferred' by the first amendment of the nation's Constitution: "Congress shall make no law respecting an establishment of religion, or prohibiting the free exercise thereof. . . ."

Likewise Canada has the freedom of conscience principle where individual prayer is allowed because it is covered under freedom of speech. Children may pray as long as they are not engaged in school activities or other instructional time. So, organized prayer at school is prohibited. In general, teachers are allowed to talk about and teach about religious holidays but cannot promote or celebrate a particular holiday.

Nevertheless, children of immigrants can be caught up in awkward situations at school. Non-Christian children can be under pressure to conform, particularly at private schools. If parents want their children to celebrate their own religious holidays, such as Eid for Muslims or Holi for Hindus, the teacher or principal will have to be approached about granting the child permission to take the day off. It is advisable to instruct younger children not to get baited into a debate trying to justify their faith at school. Children can also be excused from a particular class if the child's religious belief clashes with the class activity.

NOTES

1. Frank Newport, "Americans More Likely to Believe in God Than the Devil, Heaven More Than Hell," Gallup News Service, June 13, 2007, http://www.gallup.com/poll/27877/Americans-More-Likely-Believe-God-Than-Devil-Heaven-More-Than-Hell.aspx.

2. "Gallup Poll Shows Democrats and Independents Less Likely to Believe in God," Coalition for America, http://election08.secular.org/node/56.

3. Paul Spoerry, "People with Higher IQs Are Less Likely to Believe in God, According to a New Study," PaulSpoerry.com, June 13, 2008, http://www.paulspoerry.com/2008/06/13/intelligent-people-less-likely-to-believe-in-god/.

4. A. J. Arberry, *Sufism* (London: Allen & Irwin, 1963), 12.

5. Karen Armstrong, *A history of God* (New York: Alfred A. Knopf, 1994), 230. Quoted in http://www.sufijalalani.com/sufism.html.

6. Sufijalalani.com, http://www.sufijalalani.com.

7. Khalil Gibran, *The Prophet* (New York: Alfred A Knopf, 1993), 80.

8. L.M. Jacobs, K. Burns, J.B. Bennett, Trauma Death: Views of the Public and Trauma Professionals on Death and Dying from Injuries," *Archives of Surgery* 143.8 (2008): 730-735.

Epilogue: The Journey to America and What I Found

"Only those who hate their own self, family, and culture, can want to abandon them. To become American, it must be I who becomes American. My Latin spirit must survive, because it is part of me. I want to maintain my culture, the importance of friendship, the expression of affection, and the sense of history, common among Latins, and essential for progress."[1]

The reasons for immigrants coming to the U.S. are numerous: economic opportunity, professional opportunity, religious and political freedom, personal relationships with residing family members, and marriage. I had no close family members in the U.S. It most definitely was not about money. My parents were very comfortable financially. It was about building a better future for my family, professional advancements, and an opportunity to excel without fear of intimidation or retaliation by religious bigots, encouraged by governmental forces and tolerated by a complicit judiciary.

Like millions of immigrants before me, I wanted to escape the suffocation that comes with growing up as part of a small minority in an intolerant culture. America was my destiny, and I could not get enough of everything American: Rock Hudson and Sandra Day movies, Tom Mix and Roy Rogers western comics, and Raymond Burr and David Janssen as *Perry Mason* and *The Fugitive*, respectively. Peggy Lee belted out "Fever" and Elvis Presley crooned "Crying in the Chapel" as I dreamed of this blessed land. Among millions across the world, I shared in the sorrow of President John F. Kennedy's tragic death. If you are like me, you saw America as this large, beautiful shining planet that represented freedom, tolerance, and generosity, and was inhabited by brave, plain speaking citizens who would not only defend their land but fought to liberate suppressed voices throughout the world. America beckoned me, and I came.

My story may not be very different from yours in terms of destiny having its sway with events. I had successfully passed the examination required of international medical graduates that was needed before a physician could apply for a training position at a U.S. hospital. I applied to the usual places in the United Kingdom and, in addition, since I did not have any relatives or close friends anywhere, picked a few random places in the U.S.

During the application process, war broke out between the country where I was a citizen and a neighboring country. All physicians were required to get a "no objection" certificate from the armed forces prior to leaving the country. In other words, you were to serve the country unless you had a good medical reason, or you knew someone high up. I was fairly sure I would be rejected for service in the armed forces. I did not know of any religious minority serving in any sensitive branch of the government. I was curious to see how that would play out. My physical examination conducted by the military doctors went very well. I was healthy, on no medications, and did not have any physical defects.

When the doctor saw my name prior to the last stop on the way out, he hesitated, then asked me to do a few sit-ups. I thought, "I bet I know what's coming up."

Sure enough, he listened to my heart and with a long face announced, "Did you know you have a heart murmur?"

Matching the long face, I replied, "No, sir."

I was then before the colonel at the exit desk, who proceeded to give me the piece of paper I really wanted, stating that the military had no objection to my leaving the country.

I signed the first contract I received, from a hospital in Atlanta and mailed it back. Since it was December, and the job started January 1, I knew I would be late. I managed to wrap up my internship at the local hospital and boarded my first intercontinental flight in late January. My father had given me $3000 and some change to start a new life. The immigration officer looked at my contract and said, "Your contract date was January 1. I cannot let you in since it is now January 28." With all the confidence I could muster, I replied, "Oh! The medical director, Dr. Glenn, said that was fine. He is still holding the job open for me." After a second look at me, he let me in. Naturally, I had not spoken to Dr. Glenn or anyone about my late arrival.

I used some of the change at John F. Kennedy International Airport, but not the way I was supposed to use it. My father had given me a phone number of someone he knew in New York. I was to call and ask for advice. I picked up the public phone and dialed the operator. I told her which number I wished to call. She mentioned an amount over $1 to put in before I was to be connected. I put the amount in, but the operator kept insisting that she showed no money had been put in the coin slot. Just as firmly I kept insisting otherwise.

She finally said "How many quarters have you put in?" I looked at the $1 bill that was stuck firmly in the coin slot, quietly hung up the phone and walked away in embarrassment.

My flight from New York landed at Hartsfield Airport in Atlanta on a cool January evening in 1972. Not being familiar with the means of transportation, an empathic security agent noticed my confusion and offered to take me to my destination if I would wait until his shift was over. His yellow Volkswagen dropped me off at the emergency room entrance after midnight. The hospital staff was not expecting a disheveled foreigner dragging an old suitcase, since my contract date had passed a month before. My first American lesson of writing a note of thanks was learned the next day. Like most immigrants from non-European countries, I had never written such a note or card. In the morning, I was given the job of a new intern on the surgical ward. My journey in American medicine had begun.

It is important that your children know about your experiences and struggles. Immigration is a traumatic event. The immigrant is uprooted from his or her surroundings and in most cases left to sink or swim with little assistance other than support from a few new acquaintances. *Culture shock* is more than an expression. It is real.

In psychological terms, there is a mourning process associated with immigration. The term *emotional refueling* has been used to describe the relationship between the immigrant and the "motherland."[2] Every immigrant refuels by either returning to the native country if possible (extramural refueling) or receiving support from relatives or new friends from the same community (intramural refueling). We go to festivals, gatherings, movies, and music concerts associated with our home country as often as we can.

Although your children will listen to your own unique story when they are young, they probably do not want to listen to repeated references to how you only had two dollars in your pocket and how you are worth a lot now due to your hard work. But, some context is necessary for them to comprehend the isolation and the yearning for parents, relatives, and friends you left behind to make a better future for you and your children.

I used most of the cash my father gave me to purchase a truly American classic, a V-8 Chevrolet Nova. A senior nurse took charge of my acclimatization ordeal and later became godmother to my children. I learned the meaning of such terms as *ten-four, give me sugar,* a *tad,* you *suck,* and *gross.* If you do not have immediate relatives or friends when you come to the U.S., it is common for someone to offer assistance especially in smaller communities. If your parents are not here, the children need surrogate grandparents, uncles and aunts. Friendly neighbors or co-workers should be taken up on offers to help you and become part of your family.

This was my America, and it gave me opportunity. I took advantage of friends, neighbors, and co-workers who offered to guide me and my family. Yes, I did have to fight discrimination at work, but this made me work harder to outdo my cohorts as a matter of necessity, pride, and to some degree, payback. But, I never doubted that the system would eventually work, and I never lost faith in God and myself.

Things changed, however, over the next three decades. Like other immigrants in the 1970s, I was raised to regard my parents as the ultimate authority on this planet. Heaven lay under a mother's feet. Teachers were next in the line of authority and were absolutely to be obeyed. Patriotism and duty to one's country and family came before any individual goals. Marriage was sacred, and divorce was not an option. The value of any human life, including the unborn, was supreme. Saving for a rainy day was emphasized over immediate gratification. Debt was to be paid back at any cost. You took responsibility for your actions. Disciplining your children was your responsibility, not transferable to proxies. Educating your children was what you gave your children as your legacy. Helping your neighbors was a duty. Assisting the poor and down-trodden was a moral imperative. Physicians were healers and not unwilling targets for harassment and lawsuits. Modesty was greatly appreciated.

These were values I tried to instill in my children, but, headwinds blew more strongly against us as time passed. I do not doubt that it will become even harder for future immigrants, at least with regard to what used to be considered traditional American values. I have continued to observe the changes in my adopted country for the past thirty-five years with some trepidation. How did the principles of the greatest generation get altered so drastically in the transition to the baby boomers, the x-generation and the millennials? Had my America abandoned me, or was my vision distorted and filtered through unrealistic expectations established by fictional characters? Where was my America?

You have observed what I am about to relate if you see the news, read the newspaper, and surf the Internet. You are worried about how your children will turn out. You should be. America records more than ninety thousand rapes annually and leads the world in this category. There were more than 40 million abortions in the thirty three years after the U.S. Supreme Court legalized abortion in 1973 through 2006. Most immigrant children are in an education system that tolerates mediocrity and looks the other way with schools that promote high school children who cannot read. This is despite spending of as much as $9000 per pupil. To make things worse, on average, about twenty-eight out of every one thousand teachers are reported to be the victims of rape, sexual assault, robbery, or aggravated assault. Any crime against a school teacher would probably be considered grave in your native country, even if the teacher was at fault.

Politicians in underdeveloped countries are often crooked. What is different to the U.S. is that politicians promote class warfare, pitting those considered rich against the middle class. Instead of rewarding hard work, the same politicians buy votes with a culture of dependency. An increasing percentage of the people, manipulated by politicians, seek special rights and privileges for more and more groups. The politicians slice and dice the population by gender, race, ethnic origin, disability, and sexual orientation until the citizenry is nothing but a set of special interest sub groups, each trying to out duel the others for government favors.

Like all legal immigrants, I stood in line to come. Why is it that we do not have the courage to have people get in an orderly line, when and if America decides which new citizens it wants to enter its sovereign borders? Why cannot we find a humane solution to the problem?

America has the highest percentage of obese people in the world. Teenage pregnancy and drug addiction risk our newborns. One of the first things immigrants are struck by when we first come to the U.S. is the size of food portions served in restaurants.

We have the highest rate of children born out of wedlock and teenage births. This is one of the scariest aspects for immigrant families. You are always wondering if your children are learning to find this behavior acceptable. Are you sure that you have persuaded them about not having premarital sex, and they understand why you will not offer them birth control advice? What if one of their friends is pregnant in high school?

At this writing, America has a divorce rate of 4.95 per 1000 people, also the highest rate in the world. How do you convince your children that the odds do not apply to you? Will your stable marriage be enough of an example that they will also make the necessary compromises and stay married?

With all the above expressions of negativity, why am I optimistic?

For me, the thought process starts with the future of immigrants in the U.S. Our success and happiness depend on the direction of our adopted country. Let me explain. It all became clear to me during the disputed national elections in 2000. My mandated preparation for the citizenship test part of the immigration interview had included reading some of the U.S. Constitution. However, my fascination during the election of 2000 led me to read more in U.S. history. The Constitution written over 200 years ago came alive and appeared to have been written just for the special circumstances. I saw the foresight of Solomon in the first ten amendments to the Constitution, the Bill of Rights, which restrict the federal government and Congress from grabbing the rights of ordinary citizens. As a Hindu, my religion teaches reincarnation.

In that context, it is entirely possible that James Madison was King Solomon reincarnated. The language is heavenly and is a model for all countries looking to empower ordinary citizens.

The most beautiful language, other than that found in religious texts, has to be the First Amendment to the Constitution, protecting the free exercise of religion, free speech, the right to assemble peacefully, and the right to petition the government. I am not aware of words articulated so simply and briefly, but yet powerfully, in any other document. Which other country has a constitution that has definitively stood the test of time?

I believe that in the long term the principles outlined in the Constitution, protected by an independent judiciary that interprets it, far outweigh any short term ups and downs. The rest of the world sees the declining dollar, Congress undercutting national security, politicians posturing to weaken the military, the declining morality, the vulnerability to energy blackmail, and borders that we do not have the will to control. The pessimists are convinced that America is a mirror image of Rome where world domination gradually turned into extinction. However, a country on the way to extinction does not lead the world in Nobel laureates (double the number of the next country the U.K.) or continue to dominate in science, technology, economics, and literature. The nation attracts some of the brightest thinkers in all disciplines. A recent Gallup poll found that 84 percent of those asked said that they are satisfied with their lives, even though periodic polls show 60 percent to 70 percent of people claim the country is headed in the wrong direction. Our life expectancy has gone from sixty-three years at birth in 1940 to an astounding seventy-eight years today. We have been blessed with enormous natural resources that we have not begun to tap.[3]

America is always the first to respond to natural disasters anywhere in the world. Generous Americans give over 3 percent of their income before taxes and increased their charitable donations significantly in 2009 to more than $300 billion, a record, according to a study released by the Giving USA Foundation. The poorest (those making under $10,000 annually) gave more as a percentage of their income than did all other groups. Of course, detractors claim this is not enough.[4]

And one more thing: We are the third most common destination for the oppressed around the world who are seeking asylum. We still attract the best minds, people looking to invent new technology, new pharmaceuticals, and new procedures. Physicians all over the world want to come to America.

I see the optimism, hope, and faith in the unique power of the individual. Alexis de Tocqueville observed that Americans were invested in individual independence, armed their women with reason and "take pride in the glory of their nation."[5] Indeed, immigrants are excited about making a contribution and raising their children to do the same. Sometimes we start at the bottom rung, but we do not remain there long. Our children have opportunities here they would never have had if we had remained in our own countries.

I see the beauty of the land, the generous spirit of the people, the sacrifices its younger citizens make to defend American values, the amazingly alive Constitution, and the faith in God. I truly see "America the beautiful."

I see the real America in my elderly patients. They are so patient, respectful, and trusting in the God that has been with them throughout their illness.

I see America in the millennial generation, which I believe is bright and is working hard to do better than their parents did. They have disadvantages. A high percentage comes from single-parent homes. I know that they will eventually understand that their parents and grandparents were decent Americans and would not leave behind an immoral, weak, cowering nation that shrinks from its duty to lead all peoples. U.S. citizens express the most pride in belonging to this country, exceeded only by Ireland. There are many, many more people in the world quietly cheering at the thought of being free from the political and religious police than there are cheering for terrorists to take over and rule their lives.

America, despite all its warts, gives suppressed people all over the world hope. Why? Because there is no other America. It is the hope that ordinary citizens will have a chance to improve their circumstances and expect their children to be more prosperous than they are. The world citizen, including the Islamic citizen, expects great things from America. That citizen is not the one you hear in the media blaming America for failures of their own corrupt and autocratic leaders. They are counting on American leadership to rise above artificial barriers of race, religion, ethnic origin, language, and geography to lead them to peace and prosperity. Immigrants have come to expect America to remain the destination of choice for others who will follow us.

Where is my America? I have faith that beneath the corrosive tarnish, the precious underpinning laid by its founders and nurtured by past generations is alive and well.

We immigrants and our children hope to help America shine.

NOTES

1. Héctor C. Sabelli, "Becoming Hispanic, Becoming American: Latin American Immigrants' Journey to National Identity" in *Immigrant Experiences: Personal Narrative and Psychological Analysis*, ed. Paul H. Elovitz and Charlotte Kahn (Cranbury, NJ: Associated University Presses, 1997), 158-179.

2. Margaret S Mahler, Fred Pine, and Anni Bergman, *The Psychological Birth of the Human Infant* (New York: Basic Books, 1975), 69.

3. See http://www.gallup.com/poll/103483/most-americans-very-satisfied-their-personal-lives.aspx.

4. See http://www.givingusa.org/press_releases/gusa/gusa060910.pdf.

Index

117